Marriage:
Fact and Fantasy

———

Ann Marsh is a trained marriage guidance counsellor. She
worked with Relate for eight years, and since 1990 has
practised privately. She started her working life as an architect. Ann has been married twice. She was widowed in her
late twenties, and then married Paddy Marsh in 1959. They
have three children and four grandchildren. Ann has lived
most of her life in London, but from 1975–1980 her family
was based at the Scargill Community in Yorkshire where
her husband was Warden and Ann worked on the chap-
laincy team. In the last few years she and Paddy have led a
number of marriage growth weekends. Ann is currently
serving as Vice-Chair on the Board of the Church Army.

—

Marriage:
Fact and Fantasy

—

Ann Marsh

First published 1994
Triangle
SPCK
Holy Trinity Church
Marylebone Road
London NW1 4DU

British Library Cataloguing in Publication Data
A catalogue record for this book is available from the British Library.
ISBN 0–281–04735–9

Typeset by Inforum, Rowlands Castle, Hants
Printed and bound in Great Britain by
BPC Paperbacks Ltd
A Member of
The British Printing Company Ltd

Contents

Foreword

The other day I heard of a wedding that cost at least £18,000. One of the guests was heard to say, 'It was like being in a dream. Everything was perfect.' The trouble is that the dream inevitably fades and gives way to realities which can feel like disappointment.

The same guest also said, 'I hope it lasts.' The higher the expectations, the greater the feeling of let-down. This is the experience of so many married couples, as counsellors and others can testify. Yet we do not like to talk about the disappointments because it can feel threatening and point at the possibility of failure. Or it can look as though we are pouring cold water on the hopes of all the well-wishers.

It is good to be hopeful. But by closing our eyes to the disturbing feelings, we remain in a dream world and can isolate each other in that world. As friends, we can leave couples 'high and dry', to work out their particular realities as they emerge, out of respect for their need for privacy. Everyone needs a measure of privacy, but as Ann Marsh reminds us, the word 'respect' means 'taking another look'.

After they are married, countless couples struggle with their own brand of the 'come-down', as fantasy turns into fact. Perhaps that is one reason why so many eschew the traditional way of getting married and settle for quieter, less formal ways of exchanging their vows. They hope to keep more in touch with reality, having seen the traditional way leaving their parents and friends with unfulfilled expectations.

We need to take another look at the gap that counsellors are filling. There is a need for both partners to acknowledge that spending time together and talking helps prevent misunderstandings, and that both are worth fighting for. Counselling needs to be regarded as a respectable tool to be used when necessary in the normal working out of a marriage at all its stages, instead of being consigned to points of crisis and breakdown. The insights of experienced accredited counsellors like Ann Marsh can provide the wisdom and weapons that we need to prevent marriages and lives breaking down.

My husband David and I married in the middle of the 1957 June heatwave in an idyllic Sussex village. Looking back, our marriage contained many of the fairy-tale elements of the perfect partnership. We were young, healthy and in love. We had supportive families and assured employment. We had not rushed into our commitment, but tested it as best we knew how, during a fifteen-month engagement. We came from homes where we had felt loved and supported. We looked forward to the future together.

During our honeymoon I was admitted to an Italian hospital with a particularly virulent strain of chicken-pox, and was isolated in a room of my own with bars at my window, in the bowels of the building. This triggered a breakdown in confidence a few weeks later. Here we found ourselves facing facts in our marriage that bothered and overwhelmed us. We were brought down to earth with a bump. The fairy-tale turned into a nightmare. Yet it was real. The facts and the fantasies fused, and we needed to sort ourselves out.

We had not bargained for the shattering of our dreams so soon after the honeymoon began. We had never discussed what we would do if either of us became ill. It did not cross our minds. Despite the promises we made about sickness and health, we were not ready to handle the emotions that

------

followed. We were both shocked. I felt guilty for being ill and upsetting things. David felt anxious and confused. While doing our best to look on the bright side, inside we were both deeply in love and at the same time deeply disappointed. We were greatly helped by talking to a doctor who encouraged us to spend more time together so that communication could continue to flow. We were enabled to untangle our threads and make a new beginning.

It would have been a help to have read a book like *Marriage: Fact and Fantasy* then. We took the doctor's advice and that early pattern has stood us in good stead. Ann Marsh had her own experience of coping with disappointment and is well placed to offer sensitive experienced guidance. If we are honest, everyone faces disappointment at some time in their marriage but not everyone knows how to handle it creatively and at an early stage. All too quickly we can resort to regretting and blaming; these are steps to despair and breakdown, until we cease to care. So why bother with marriage at all?

In the International Year of the Family in 1994 there will be much talk and thought focused on what we mean by The Family. This will inevitably raise once more the subject of marriage. The statistics are unlikely to show that the increasing trend of marriage break-up is slowing down. Yet people still want to be married, and many want to be married in church. This book is a valuable and positive Christian contribution to the debate. It springs from years of experience and from a realistic approach. But it is more than that. It is a good companion for married people, providing comfort, challenge and guidance for all who are interested in the need for marriage maintenance. Most couples set out on marriage with high hopes and good intentions. More couples need encouragement and guidance when the relationship begins to creak.

The idea that material goods can be repaired nowadays is regarded as slightly old-fashioned and out of date. We are encouraged to throw away and buy new. It is perhaps not surprising that relationships have become caught up in this thinking. Ann Marsh, and countless others, are wanting to say, 'Wait a minute, there is another way. It is worth bothering.' She reminds us that we take ourselves as individuals with us wherever we go. We are all damaged to some degree and unless we are enabled to look honestly and courageously at our own behaviour in the light of our roots, we are likely to encounter the same problems in ourselves in each new situation. We are likely to start building the same defensive wall with another person sooner or later.

So is it worth bothering with marriage? Is it more than just a slip of paper? Some of us would say a resounding yes. We say yes not because we want to boast about our good experience, but because we know how difficult it is to maintain close relationships for any length of time by ourselves, and how rewarding it can be when we can own our difficulties and work towards change. We know what a difference it has made to have been able to talk truthfully together, and know that there is further help nearby when we come up against a brick wall. We have found marriage to be a place of forgiveness and new starts, a place where we can learn about mutual respect and the reworking of self–esteem. It can be one of the primary places of growth and healing provided that we want it to be. But it involves commitment, courage and honesty.

It takes courage to admit disappointment. We find courage when we know that we are not alone. Others have been there before us. Facing the facts of our particular partnership, warts and all, is vital in avoiding the pitfalls of remaining in the fantasy world where living happily ever after involves no cost, and no other people.

Ann Marsh will have achieved her goal if this book encourages one couple towards a new openness of communication with each other. Once this begins to happen a new order can begin where the idea of maintenance and repair is not old-fashioned any longer. Instead of walls we can create bridges, and instead of frozen silences we can face each other with new hope and determination.

Grace Sheppard
Liverpool, 1994

Preface

To be human is to experience a gap between life as it is and life as we would like it to be. The same is true of marriage, but what is realistic and what is wishful thinking? This book examines some of those facts and fantasies and how they develop.

Fantasy is a word used in different ways. In terms of dictionary definitions I am using it as meaning 'imagination unrestricted by reality'. In relation to marriage this is about unreal or inappropriate expectations for one's partner or for oneself. In the chapter on sex and gender I shall touch on fantasy as 'a series of pleasing mental images serving to fulfil a need not gratified by reality', but sexual fantasy is not the subject of the book in general.

I have constantly needed a word for 'either he or she', but the English language does not have one. I have, therefore, often used the plural 'they' for adults, and 'it' for a little child. In no way, though, do I see a little child as less than a full he or she person.

In the examples I have given from other people's lives, the names and some of the personal details have been changed to preserve confidentiality. In fact many of the stories are true for more than one of the couples I have seen, so that someone may recognize their own situation in someone else's similar story. I hope that this will be so, because the whole purpose of a particular example is to highlight a more general truth.

This book is addressed to married couples or to couples whose commitment to one another feels to have the strength of a marriage vow, but much of what I have written applies to relationships in general. Whether married or single, we all enjoy relationships and we also suffer them, and walk away from them all through our lives. And whoever we are we will have some unreal expectations of ourselves and others. However, marriage often sharpens the issues, and marriage makes it more difficult for us to walk away from a situation. It is therefore within the boundaries of a shared life and home that I have looked at some of the facts and fantasies of a close relationship. My hope is that, in the difficulties I explore, this book may bring with it something of the companionship we all share as fellow human beings.

I believe that if both partners in a marriage can read this book and talk about it together, it will be much more than twice as useful as it might be to one partner. As a marriage guidance counsellor I have often seen relief come into a relationship when a partner has spelt out something which may have seemed obvious to that person, but is a revelation to their partner. It has been an 'Aha! Now I see what you are saying' experience which has created a shift, however small, in the understanding between them. My hope is that this book might create occasions for that to happen.

1

Great expectations

The Charlie Brown cartoons have an accuracy that makes me smile. 'On the great cruise of life,' says Lucy, 'some people sit in their deck chairs at the front of the boat, looking into the future, and some sit at the back, looking at where they have been. Where do you sit, Charlie Brown?' and Charlie replies, 'I can never get my deck chair open!'

In married life too, there are those who are looking ahead, trying to get a vision of where they are going, those who are looking back over what has happened to them so far and perhaps making comparisons with friends' or parents' marriages, and those who feel like Charlie Brown. Looking anywhere is a luxury they can't get into, because marriage is proving a struggle, muddle, and confusion. Maybe we have felt all three of these at different times.

The very word 'marriage' is heavily charged with emotion. So many ideas, hopes, and fears are contained in it.

Picture the wedding day, and imagine the thoughts in the minds of some of those present. Perhaps the bride's father is thinking, 'I'm so glad to have got my youngest daughter married; now I can enjoy my retirement.' The mother of the groom might wonder, 'Will he settle down? He's been such a restless boy, always wanting a change.' And maybe the bride's sister is feeling, 'She's so lucky, I should be up there. I'm the oldest, but no one expects me to get married. She's always been the prettiest.' A close family friend might be struggling with past memories and thinking, 'I do hope they can make a go of it. We didn't and God knows I tried hard enough.'

Workmates might be day-dreaming about their futures and thinking, 'They look such a wonderful couple!' Love, envy, fear, and even depression are around, and in this charged atmosphere there is an unspoken question hanging in the air, 'Will it work?' It is not surprising that many people are glad to quieten their minds with several drinks.

It is also a unique occasion. Great effort and cost may have gone into making it a day to remember. Guests crowd around the festooned car, and you overhear someone say, 'It was fantastic. I'm dying to see the photos.' Lovely affirming things are said to the couple, and they leave in style.

Bearing all this in mind — the build-up, the effort and cost, and the expectations — it is not surprising that the first negative emotion to be experienced is usually disappointment. It may be dismissed quickly from the mind, or it may linger as a vague anxiety, but there it is, an ingredient to a greater or lesser degree in every marriage. Disappointment is a difficult emotion to admit, even to oneself, let alone to one's partner, but it comes with thoughts like these: 'This isn't what I expected!' 'Does it matter?' 'Can I change it?' 'Am I trapped?' It is important that we realize just how normal these feelings are, because along with disappointment come feelings of loneliness and isolation: 'Other people haven't got this particular circumstance or attitude to deal with, they wouldn't understand.'

Judy spoke of her disappointment to me one day when she said, 'I didn't think that sport was so important to Mike. I knew he was keen on games, but he seemed more interested in "us" when we were engaged. I thought it would go on like that after we were married. I thought I was more important to him than sport!'

On another occasion Mary's husband Richard said, 'Mary's always talking to her parents on the phone. I didn't realize she was so dependent on them. She asks for their opinion before mine, and I think we should be deciding things on our own, together. Anyway, she should be able to make her own decisions without them. I didn't know she was so tied up.'

_____

Great expectations

The truth is that we all go into marriage with some fantasies about our partner, as well as about ourselves. There may have been people in our past who, we feel, have really understood us and people who have been good to us. There have been others whose way of life we admire. These have contributed to a mental image of someone who will complete us, making us feel a more fulfilled and rounded person. This picture is designed by our emotional needs. It has conscious, semi-conscious, and subconscious parts in it, and it is very precious to us. It defines what sort of a person I believe myself to be, and what sort of a partner I believe I need.

It sometimes reminds me of a toddler's jigsaw, the kind that has a country scene with little cut-outs of a house, man, woman, child, dog, and so on. Each cut-out has a little knob on it, so that you can hold the piece and wiggle it into place. We pick up our 'partner piece' and try to fit them into our own picture. We twist and turn but there seems to be too much on this side and not enough on that. Can I possibly make my partner fit? By no means, and in any case they are trying to fit me into their picture, which is designed from their unique history. It is here that the fantasies meet the facts.

Our heads may be very rational about all those first stirrings of disappointment, and say to us, 'Now the honeymoon is over, this is for real. What did you really expect? There are bound to be good times and bad times. Just get on with it.' But our emotions work differently. In our heart or, as some would say, in our guts, we hurt with the reality of disappointment, and we are afraid. We do not want to acknowledge it even to ourselves, and an inner voice says, 'Forget it – stuff it back inside – don't talk about it – for goodness' sake don't rock the boat!'

This inner voice is the voice of past experience, and it is well practised in its advice. We have learnt ways of dealing with our disappointments from our earliest years. As children we were told by our parents and teachers that they were busy people, and that was usually true. However loving their

———

intentions, they were often absent or unaware of our moments of disappointment and so we learned to push down the tears and get on with it. And now? Well, we are grown-up!

It doesn't occur to us that failing to share our disappointments with our partner is like placing a brick in a wall between us. Or it does occur to us, but the risk of sharing seems too great. And so we erect this wall together, each working silently from our own side. When things get bad we can see there is a wall between us, but we have also learnt from childhood to defend ourselves by blaming others. This means that we are likely to believe that the wall has been built largely by our partner. I am not referring here to marriages in special difficulty. This meeting of fact and fantasy and the pain of it is a normal part of any marriage journey.

We go into marriage with high hopes. It is as if on our wedding day we had a card hanging around our necks saying 'great expectations' — both those we had for ourselves and those that others had for us — and some of these expectations have met with disappointment. And then communication, sharing, closeness, the very things that seemed so good between us suddenly seem much more limited than we thought, and we get stuck. Our conversation over certain issues becomes like a scratched record, when the needle is stuck in a groove and it repeats the same phrase over and over again. 'We've had this argument before; it gets us nowhere, you always . . . we never . . .'

This sort of situation can erupt very quickly and get worse, even leading to the decision to separate, or it can more usually be a dis-ease we learn to live with, but which restricts our capacity for being loving or lovable. Either way we are likely to experience self-doubt, and say to ourselves, 'What about those ideals I brought with me into marriage, all those hopes for "us"? Were they realistic? Are they achievable or are they the stuff that dreams are made of? Is it my fault that things are not working out as I thought? What hopes are possible for us in our

———

marriage? Where are the facts in our relationship and where are the fantasies?'

It is through this minefield that I hope to walk in the following chapters. I cannot know the route through your particular field, but I can indicate some of the mines I have discovered through my own and other people's journeys. I have found marriage to be at the same time much worse and much better than I would have thought possible, both more restricting and more freeing than I would have believed. I have found within myself both a stronger hate and a stronger love than I knew about. I have found marriage to be a paradox, which often feels like a state of confusion. But paradox, that holding together of opposite truths, is at the heart of what it is to be human. We are all capable of some such loving and sacrificial acts, and some so despicable and cruel. We can be full of insight in one direction and utterly blind in another.

A friend once said to me, 'Truth is a very large parcel. Our arms are stretched wide apart in trying to hold it, and our hands have to push in opposite directions.' So too with marriage. We are stretched as we try to contain the 'us' of our marriage and we also know about the times we push against one another.

My work as a marriage guidance counsellor has been both in the secular world, and within the Christian church and so some people who have shared their experiences with me have come from a religious background, or brought with them a commitment to the Christian faith. For them their personal agenda and fears can collide with another agenda, coming from their understanding of the standards and teaching of Christ. Sometimes our religious faith can be used in an unhealthy way to defend us from looking at the truth about ourselves. Sometimes it can liberate us from old patterns of self-doubt and guilt and give us courage and hope on our journey.

I remember a husband in his late twenties whose parents had been very ambitious for him, and he had not reached their expectations for him in his career as an accountant. Henry's father worked for a major city company, but Henry was doing a much more lowly job as an administrative assistant. However, he had married a wife who represented all that his father had hoped for his son. She became the professionally-qualified and competent daughter-in-law working for a well-known firm. The 'couple' now contained enough to please his parents, or so he felt. But while Veronica was Henry's achievement — to have attracted and married that kind of girl — she was also a threat to him, a constant reminder of what he was not, and this was immensely painful.

In his distress, Henry latched on to St Paul's teaching about the husband being the head of the wife, and, taking it out of context, he was using it to beat his wife down to a position lower than his own. Their marriage was in great need of help but he dismissed further counselling with me as being 'not Christian enough'. I had touched a raw nerve that was too painful even to examine.

But another Christian couple, who came to see me after the husband had had a brief affair with a mutual friend, were able together, with God and with each other, to face the reality about their relationship. They began to look back over the ways in which they had both failed each other. They came to see that they had some joint responsibility for what had happened, and through the pain of their honesty, and faith in the forgiving love of God, they found a way to forgive one another. This was not a one-off statement about 'I forgive you', but a process of healing as each partner learned to accept and love themselves and each other for what they were. I see in these two illustrations a negative and a positive use of Christian teaching.

In my own journey of life I have experienced two marriages, both completely different. Peter, my first husband, suffered from multiple sclerosis. It was in its very early stages when we married. I was twenty-two, and in my last year of training as an architect. Peter was working as an engineer/designer from home. The disease slowly worsened, though with some good remission periods, and he died, following a minor bladder operation, after we had had eight years together. His last few years were spent in a wheelchair, and I was the breadwinner, and so the marriage had its own peculiar set of circumstances. In this relationship, as I look back, I know that we met each other's needs at the time in a very particular way, but it would take another book to describe how this was so.

In my second marriage, Paddy and I have experienced the more normal stresses of life, around such issues as children, money, sex, in-laws and religion. As I write drawing on my own experience, I am very conscious that much of it is not my story but ours. The fact that Paddy is giving me his encouragement and support is his own contribution to this book. To say that I couldn't have written it without him is in one sense obvious, but is also true at a much deeper level. The 'me' that writes is the outcome of the 'us' of the thirty-two years of our married life, and our own marriage has been the ground for much of my thinking.

In the following chapters I hope to show some of the ways in which the fantasies we have about ourselves and our partners have established themselves in us. I shall look at some of the problems these create, and the process of changing our fantasies into realities. I shall look at how relationships get stuck and unstuck, and at the ways in which the problems we talk about are often a cover for deeper issues which seem too hot to handle. I shall make a plea for more honest and open communication between couples, even when that seems risky. I hope to convey something of the surprise and joy that can come through gradually uncovering the real person in each other.

2

The seed-bed of our emotions

The childhood shows the man,
As the morning shows the day
Milton[1]

In the first chapter I mentioned the personal world which each
of us brings into marriage. Now I want to look more closely at
what we learned in those early years of childhood.

When I am with a couple who want to look at their marriage together, it is not long before either I or they will mention their parents. Sometimes one will add, 'I had a reasonably
happy childhood and my parents are good people.' Often I feel
that they are also giving me an unspoken message, which runs
something like this: 'Don't you dare criticize my parents, that's
what all these psychological types do. They tell you it's your
parents' fault and I don't buy that one. This is our problem and
you can leave them out of it.'

But we can't, because our parents are our roots. And criticism
is not the issue. The point is not primarily about good or bad
parenting, although of course that comes into it, but about what
it means to be a member of the human race. When the Psalmist
wrote, 'In sin did my mother conceive me', he was not saying
that he had a bad mother, or that sex is evil, but that each
generation is affected by the deprivation, ignorance, and selfish-
ness of the previous generation. When Moses said that 'the sins
of the fathers [for which read parents!] are visited on the children unto the third and fourth generation', he was not making a
threat, he was describing a fact of life. That is the way it is.

The clinical work done by the psychiatrist, the late Dr Frank Lake,[2] convinced him that babies in the womb register the emotions of their mother. But even if that were not so, we can see with our own eyes that from birth onwards a baby picks up the atmosphere in which he lives. He does not understand it, but he absorbs the feeling like blotting paper. He has no power to do otherwise in those earliest years. The bad experiences are 'visited' on us as babies and we are 'trespassed against'.

Parents are sometimes unaware of the messages they are giving to their children. I have heard mothers talking in a supermarket queue or on the phone and saying things about their own children in their presence, as if the children were deaf or could not possibly understand. Like the mother who said, 'Tom is painfully shy. He never joins in with the games at parties like the other children, do you, Tom? I don't know what to do with him.' Poor Tom, publicly classified and condemned. How much harder it will be for him now to grow out of that shyness, yet the conversation came out of parental concern. Of course it is equally true that we are affected by the loving-kindness and creativity that is visited on us, and also passed from grandparents to parents to ourselves and our children.

There is an endless debate about how much of our character is due to our inborn nature and how much is from our nurture and environment. There is an equally hot debate about how much choice we have as human beings, and to what extent we are programmed by our past. But whatever our opinions most of us feel in our bones that being human involves us in having a power of choice and using it.

Jews and Christians see themselves as being made in the image of God, meaning by this that human beings share with him the capacity to be creative, to love, and to make choices. We do all this, of course, within the limitations of our character and upbringing. In looking at our roots, we are looking at the soil out of which we have grown and, though local ingredients will vary a great deal, the soil is common to us all, living as we do in an imperfect world.

In marriage we engage with emotions to do with loving and believing ourselves to be lovable. These reach down to early feelings both about dependency and feeling trapped, and about seeing ourselves as powerful or weak. As we stir up feelings about love, we uncover anger and hateful feelings, and an unsureness about being close to or separate from those we love. It is rather like playing with a stick in a pond, and seeing the clear water become muddied by the debris from the bottom. We cannot know the shape of the original matter which now forms the sludge, but we can see its effect on the surface of the water.

Here is an example of a fairly common feeling shared by married couples, which comes from our very earliest experience. I shall call it 'the bliss of being known'. During the first year of life, the baby is not really a separate being. It is tied, as it were, by an umbilical cord of sight and sound and touch to its mother (or mother figure). It cannot think 'I am'. It cannot talk, or walk or make its needs known without someone being there who is for that child 'all-knowing', someone who can anticipate the needs it has, to be fed, clothed, cleaned, comforted, held, and loved. In no way can the baby make itself acceptable. It has to be accepted just as it is, whether wet and windy or cooing with delight. In the earliest months it can ask for nothing except by tears. When the baby is miserable, it experiences those feelings from the top of its head to the end of its toes. It is 'in a state', we say, and the state is misery. Conversely, when the baby has been fed and is dry, warm, and comfortable, and being smiled upon, it can experience a state of bliss, a completeness of well-being from head to toe.

Each of us was once that baby. And those moments of bliss, be they few or many, remain on our subconscious memory tape

---

all our life. One important characteristic that draws us to another person is that with them we feel, 'Here is someone with whom I can be at rest.' We can be silent in each other's company and feel understood. We can relax in each other's arms.

Sometimes your partner says just what you were thinking, or realizes you need something before you ask, and you feel wonderfully known and cared for. But when that unconscious memory of being known and loved stirs within us, it sets up its own demands and we begin to feel about our partner, 'If you really loved me, you would know how I feel, or what I need and when I need it, without my having to ask.' It is then that we have touched fantasy, for there is no way that one adult can be all-knowing to another. We have had separate lives and thoughts, most of which are unknown to our partner. But the reawakening of the good moments has stirred the longing for what might have been.

I remember a typical conversation between a couple in which the wife said, 'But why don't you do it? Surely you know what I like!' And her husband said, 'I'm not psychic. How can I know what you want? You never said.' It is here that we have to build a relationship by talking and sharing together. Whilst still enjoying those moments of feeling known and understood when they occur, we have to recognize that at other times we shall need to ask for what we want. We will need to say what we like and open ourselves up to the other person so that they can know us better. Then they will know what being loved means for us in that particular situation.

We may also have to repeat those needs to our partner, because they will forget. Our deep needs are not burnt into their souls from childhood, as ours have been. Theirs may be as great but not quite the same.

The sense of bliss at being known and understood is reflected on in Psalm 139, written nearly three thousand years ago:

O LORD, you have searched me and you know me . . .
Before a word is on my tongue you know it
   completely, O Lord . . .
Such knowledge is too wonderful for me . . .
   You knit me together in my mother's womb . . .
   Your eyes saw my unformed body . . .
   How precious to me are your thoughts, O God!
   How vast is the sum of them![3]

These lines were a very special help to Tony, a man we met in his thirties. He had been born illegitimate and brought up in a harsh orphanage. He told us that he had recently become aware of God's love for him. He had realized that God had known him in the womb, and therefore knew all about the difficulties he had battled with in his childhood. This had given him a new security at the very place where he had known none.

But every penny has two sides. For each of us, the security of having our baby needs known and met brought with it equally strong negative feelings. These came to us in the moments of panic when our needs were not understood, and in moments of desolation at being alone and in need. Dependency is a thing we experience as a very mixed blessing, to say the least, and the baby in us all has experienced feelings ranging from heaven to hell.

When the baby's cries were not heard, and maybe hunger pangs called in the stomach, or painful wind, dependence brought with it emotions of rage and panic. The fact is that any baby that is unattended for long enough will actually die and so its dependence is total and 'aweful'.

Something of that same sense of abandonment and anger can be touched when we share life together and become inter-dependent on one another. It may be triggered off by the simplest of things such as one partner not paying a cheque into the bank account, or not ironing a shirt, or forgetting to post a

------

letter. But a partner can experience a sense of outrage which is out of all proportion to the event, and feel let down and unloved.

Perhaps you feel that I am overstating the case. But I want to show that in some of our moments of intense irritation we are picking up an echo from the past which is very real for us but which leaves our partner reeling and feeling how unfair we are being. All of us will have good and bad memories of being dependent and these will be triggered off in what seems a random way. Our partner will feel that we are being irrational, and so we are in relation to the event in question, but the reasons are there, back in our past experience.

I can think of a boy brought up with a mentally handicapped sister who had often felt at the mercy of her violent and 'stupid' behaviour. He married a girl who was a great enthusiast for causes and would get quite worked up when she spoke about them. He could not stand her when she was like that and would say that she was 'over the top'. He felt frightened and thought others would see her as ridiculous. His slight feelings of present embarrassment were picking up on his past panic.

Some people get extremely anxious when they expect their partner back home at a certain time and he or she does not appear until an hour or so later. They can experience sweat and panic, and when their partner finally arrives they are furious at the pain he or she has 'caused' them. But maybe that pain was created long ago by being left crying in a cot, or left waiting for Mum to come back from work, and their tolerance has already been stretched too far. When fears like these can be shared and the pain can be believed in and respected by a partner, then a process of gradual healing can often take place over the past hurt, even if it cannot be traced to its original cause. But it calls for the kind of discussion in which blaming is put on one side, and each partner listens to and values the feelings of the other. In order for this to happen the heat has to be taken out of the occasion, but we will come to this in a later chapter.

Mixed feelings about being independent are closely linked to a similar ambivalence a baby discovers as it explores its own power over people. Have you seen a baby in a high chair pushing a toy to the edge of the tray and watching it drop on to the floor? The adult picks it up and gives it back. The baby does it again, and again. He begins to feel that he has power to get the adult to respond. The baby grins, and you sense that he is enjoying himself. It is a new experience to have some control over an adult and the power feels good.

But picture another scene, a three-year-old squabbling with a younger brother. They pull the telephone on to the floor, and then upset the wastepaper basket. Today the washing-machine has gone wrong and the hot tap is running into a sink full of clothes. The water starts to overflow on to the floor and the mother rushes to turn it off. The younger brother is now scribbling on the three-year-old's favourite story-book and she snatches it in fury from him and pushes him over. He screams. The mother then screams at the three-year-old, 'You're driving me mad, the pair of you.' She sits down with her head in her hands and burst into tears. How does the three-year-old feel then? She believes that she has made her mother cry. She has done that to a powerful grown-up. She didn't realize that she had that power and she is frightened by the apparent destructiveness of it.

We also need to bear in mind that young children have not yet learnt to distinguish between the thoughts in their head and the deeds they do. It takes a while for them to learn what it means to tell a lie. As they watch the pantomime of *Peter Pan* they will obey as the compère encourages them to shout 'we believe in fairies' just in case Tinkerbell will die if they don't. Their thoughts might make it happen.

All children will have angry thoughts about those close to them, feeling jealous, misunderstood or left out at times, or just

———

wanting to assert themselves. A child may shout at a brother, 'I'll kill you if you don't give that back to me', and this reflects the force of those feelings, quite murderous at that moment. These are normal emotions which we learn to handle as we grow up, but if something bad happens to that brother, the other child may feel a sense of guilt about having had such destructive thoughts, believing that in some way they helped the bad to happen. In the event of a family death or illness, or divorce, there will be many unspoken guilty feelings among those concerned, but children will often take to themselves a blame which is quite inappropriate. My youngest daughter demonstrated this very clearly to me when she was seven years old.

My widowed father, aged eighty-three, was living with us when Jane was born, and he died when she was six. After her brother and sister had started school, for three years she and my father and I used to have lunch together every day. My father came from an age when children were kept firmly in their place, 'seen but not heard', and he was always awkward and gruff with children. Our lunchtime conversation was punctuated with remarks like: 'Jane, don't talk with your mouth full', 'Jane, don't interrupt your mother', 'Sit still', 'Be quiet', and so on. I had been frightened of my father as a child, and some of that fear stopped me from being protective enough towards Jane. In the year following my father's death Jane's behaviour became more difficult. One day my husband, Paddy, came back from work at lunchtime to pick up the car and I remarked to Jane, 'It's a long time since we've had someone to lunch on a school day, not since Grandpa was with us. Do you remember Grandpa?' She nodded. 'He was very fond of you', I said. 'I know', Jane answered. 'He used to watch me on the climbing frame.' 'Do you remember any presents he gave you?' 'Yes, he gave me a manicure set when I stopped biting my fingernails, but don't go on about Grandpa. I know he loved me, but I didn't love him enough so he shrivelled up and died.'

———

17

This incident convinced me more than anything else of the truth that children believe their thoughts can kill, and you can't feel much more powerful than that! After this incident I talked about Grandpa to Jane saying how difficult I too had found him and how hard it must have been for Jane when he had kept telling her off. I explained that at ninety his body was worn out, and that was why he had died. There followed several conversations about Grandpa in the following weeks. Jane's behaviour became much more relaxed and she settled down at school. Had all this not arisen, Jane might still be carrying a vague unidentifiable guilt about her own destructiveness in that situation. She had also, of course, experienced a sense of great weakness in being unable to voice any of her anger at being continually put down.

In my conversations with couples we uncover many confused feelings which have their origins in childhood events, but perhaps the most important of all are those related to love and hate. What does it mean to be loving or lovable? St John says in his epistle, 'Herein is love, not that we love God, but that he loved us.'[4] We have to be loved to know about love, and that first love comes to the baby from the parents. And it was in relation to them that we first experienced unmet need, anger and moments of hate. But what could we do with our unlovable thoughts and our 'baby' anger and hate?

Certainly every child has angry and destructive feelings, but there is a great risk involved in expressing them too strongly. A child senses that if it bites the hand that feeds, it puts its own security at risk. So it learns to suppress the full force of those feelings in order to preserve the feeling of having a 'good' mother. Those 'bad' feelings get pushed down inside or pushed out on to other people or things — repressed and projected. We need to preserve the good 'knight' or 'fairy godmother' in our parents, and not the 'ogre' or the 'witch' in them. In fact we use fairy stories, cops and robbers, cowboys and Indians, as a way of giving vent to

———

some of these strong subconscious feelings. We detach them or split them off from the person who first evoked them. We may even blame ourselves rather than put our own security in them at risk.

In some families any expression of anger is frowned upon, and anger in children is severely punished, while in others one parent's anger may engender a lot of fear. But whatever the cause, for some children the fear of expressing their own angry thoughts is so great that they grow up quite unable to do so. In fact they can become quite unaware that such feelings exist in them. Then along comes a close adult relationship, with a growing sense of closeness and interdependence, and the repressed feelings start to bubble up inside like activated yeast in too small a container, pushing the lid off.

If this has been our experience, we find ourselves using a lot of emotional energy in trying to keep the lid on. We get depressed and drained and our anxiety grows at the out-of-controlness' of those feelings. We fear that in unguarded moments the lid will fly off and the yeast will spill all over the floor. As our panic rises, we become violent and abusive, and find that the lid has in fact come off. We have lost control; we whom everyone thought to be so mild and gentle.

'I was a very patient man until we had children', a father said to me. 'The kids really get to me and I lose my cool and go wild.' C.S. Lewis in *Mere Christianity*[5] likens those feelings to rats in the cellar of our personality which prefer to live in the dark. If someone opens the door on them, they scurry in all directions looking for cover. So we like to be in control of the door, so that there will be time for the rats to hide. Children often cause the door to fly open. They don't create the feelings, but they do expose them.

What does the baby learn from the parent about loving and being lovable? At best, a sense of acceptance, and of precious worth; ways of showing kindness and caring for another person; a sense of freedom to explore and experiment, to make mistakes and to tolerate their own and other people's limitations and differences.

But along with that come some conflicting messages. A.A. Milne in his book of poems, *Now We Are Six*, captures something of this confusion in 'The Good Little Girl':[6]

> It's funny how often they say to me, 'Jane?
> Have you been a *good* girl?'
> 'Have you been a *good* girl?'
> And when they have said it, they say it again,
> 'Have you been a *good* girl?'
> 'Have you been a *good* girl?'
>
> I go to a party, I go out to tea,
> I go to an aunt for a week at the sea,
> I come back from school or from playing a game;
> Wherever I've come from, it's always the same:
> 'Well?
> Have you been a *good* girl, Jane?'

And then Jane goes to the zoo and gets the same response and the poem ends:

> Well, what did they think that I went there to do?
> And why should I want to be bad at the Zoo?
> *And should I be likely to say if I had?*
> So that's why it's funny of Mummy and Dad,
> This asking and asking, in case I was bad,
> 'Well?
> Have you been a *good* girl, Jane?'

Jane is struggling with the feeling that being 'good', and therefore lovable, is conditional on her being very passive towards grown-ups, and not causing them any trouble or making her presence felt. You can hear in the last verse the gulf between Jane's excitement of going to the zoo and her frustration with her parents' priorities and seeming lack of imagination. Being lovable almost seems to rob her of her enjoyment of life.

Love can sound even more obviously conditional: 'If you are good you can go to the fair.' 'If you pass that exam I'll buy you a bike.' It looks as if we will have to earn it, so it begins to feel that love is more about what we do than what we are.

Love also makes us open to be hurt. Your best friend at school moves away and you feel bereft. Or someone you love, or even a pet, dies. We soon find out that loving makes us vulnerable to pain and loss. We can feel a lot of hurt when our words or deeds are misunderstood. Perhaps we said something nice to a friend or teacher and a mate said, 'You just said that to suck up. You are a creep!' and that may not have been true. In those moments we feel very unloved.

And so gradually the child learns the boundaries and conditions of love and tries to avoid hurt wherever possible. By trial and error we learn when and with whom it is safe to share our feelings, and we create a safe distance between ourselves and those we love, which protects us and helps us to develop our own identity.

When we marry we are inviting someone to come inside that boundary, and once again childhood fears are aroused. How close is close enough? Will my idea of a close relationship be the same as my partner's? People often speak of feeling pushed away when they want to be close, or clutched at when they feel the need for space. And what does it mean to care for another person? How do we express it? In all of this we will be reactivating messages from the past about what it meant to us to be loving or lovable.

I am reminded of a time early in my own marriage when I used to say to Paddy as he was going out, 'I think it will get colder today. I should take a coat', or 'It looks like rain. I would take an umbrella.' Paddy would make some obviously irritated reply implying 'Don't fuss me!' My own mother was short on fussiness. If I got a cold it was my fault for not having taken a coat, so she said. Paddy's mother fussed him. He had been seriously ill with scarlet fever at the age of two and had nearly died, and he felt that she was always trying to wrap him up in cotton wool. My remark to Paddy was caring for him in the way that I would have liked to have experienced. His reply to me was saying, 'I've had too much of that, and it makes me feel like a child.'

This may seem a trivial example, but it does show the hidden influence of the past on the present. With our discovery of the seed-bed of those particular reactions came opportunity to learn about each other, and to avoid the irritation. In fact it was several years before we recognized the reasons behind that particular small but irritating exchange. We have all forgotten many of our childhood experiences, but our emotional reactions bear their stamp.

3

The choice of a partner

None of us can really put into words what made us choose our own partner, even though the reasons were strong enough for us to decide to share our lives. We can be even more lost for words when some of our friends get married. We say, 'I can't see what she sees in him — or he in her.' The reasons are there, but they will come from a mixture of unconscious and semi-conscious drives, and meet hidden needs as well as the obvious ones. I believe that this is true for couples who co-habit as well as for those who have chosen to marry.

Though there are couples who have come together by complete chance, more usually we meet on some sort of common ground. It may have been back at school, or college, or we may share the same career or workplace. Sometimes we meet through clubs, or attend the same place of worship. This common ground, which forms the basis of most friendships, is an important element in marriage. Later into married life, as children arrive and careers develop, the common ground will often shift from, say, the sports club to the house or garden, but doing things together and being together socially with other people is still as important to us; we are social creatures.

In the first few months of going out with someone as a couple, we begin to share ourselves. Then we may become conscious of how much the other person means to us, and we try to communicate this to them. It may be with words or actions, but we want them to know that we find them both loving and lovable. If they respond in a similar way, we become aware of feelings of unity in one another which are beyond words to express. Maybe we find that these are only reached by poetry, or in the words of a song, or in the silence of each other's arms. The relationship has now changed from being 'just friends' to the sharing of ourselves with another person at a deeper level. An attraction is there that is more than a physical sexual feeling, though it includes this. It feels powerful yet inexplicable. There is a line in the old song about meeting a stranger 'across a crowded room', and feeling an instant attraction, and this is not pure sentimentality.

Robin Skynner, founder member of the Institute of Family Therapy, describes an exercise in his book *Families and How to Survive Them*,[1] which he uses on training courses with new groups of trainees who are strangers to one another. They are asked to mill about the room in silence, and then choose a partner who reminds them of someone in their family, or who gives them the feeling that they would have 'filled a gap' in their family. Then the pairs compare notes to see if they can find out why they picked each other. In the second stage of the exercise they find another couple and are asked to make an imaginary family, agreeing together who shall take which role. They find, in fact, that they have in some way created a family with a number of similarities to their own.

The 'connectedness' between people has been picked up out of the air, so it seems, but it is actually communicated in a multitude of unspoken ways. These can include gestures, ways of sitting or standing, clothing, facial expression, and even the lines on the face. There is something familiar about that person and they therefore feel safer and in some way knowable. It even happened on one occasion that several people who were very slow to 'partner' and 'make a family' found that they had in common a background of having been fostered or adopted.

Occasionally I have looked at a society magazine in a waiting room; the kind which has a page of photographs of recently-married couples. It has made me smile to see how often the pairs look so alike in facial features or bone structure that they could easily be taken for brother and sister.

I have taken part in similar exercises to Skynner's myself, and am convinced that we have a subconscious awareness of someone with similar emotional experiences and needs to our own and that this plays a large part in our choice of a marriage partner. The following accounts give two such instances.

Geoffrey and Hannah had very different families as children, but in both there was a factor which made them feel that they were expected to fill the role of a child of the opposite sex. Geoffrey was the oldest of three boys. When he was three his mother had twins, and Geoffrey was no longer the child his mother could play with and enjoy. She was up to her eyes with two demanding babies. One way he did get attention was to be Mummy's Little Helper, and this made him feel close and appreciated. He knew, too, that his mother often wished she had had a girl. The pattern continued, so that as an adult he was still the one to help his mother with the vegetables for Sunday lunch, though resenting the twins' way of opting out. He felt pushed into what felt like the more feminine role.

Hannah was the younger of two girls. Her parents had lost a boy before Hannah was born. No doubt they grieved very much for this lost son, and in some way Hannah was the replacement child. She grew up with a feeling of being second-best, and a disappointment to her parents however hard she tried to please them. She had found it hard, too, to enjoy feeling feminine. Her sister, whom she felt was cleverer, seemed to have the valued daughter's role in the family. Hannah wanted very much to feel close to her father, but it was her sister and father who had intelligent conversations at dinner, while she and her mother sat in silence. Geoffrey and Hannah shared a background of being displaced persons, who were filling in for someone of the opposite sex.

Chris and Ruth also had a lot in common. Chris had been sent away to boarding-school in Britain, because his father's job meant that his parents had to live in India. He was six years old when he went away, and during the first term he cried and cried. However, he soon learnt that it didn't pay to express his true feelings there. His time at school was not happy, and there was a lot of latent anger in him towards his parents. But how could he express that to them in the brief holiday spells which were such a welcome break?

Ruth had been sexually abused by her two older brothers since she was three. When she was old enough she tried to tell her mother, but to her dismay she was not believed. A brother said on one occasion, 'She's lying. I was just tickling her and romping about on the bed.' Ruth and Chris both shared the feeling that their parents didn't care enough about them to find out the truth of their situation, and protect them. They both felt abused and neglected, and they picked out someone with the same hurt.

When we find someone with similar emotional needs to our own, they are likely to seem very sympathetic towards us. Obviously this feels good, and gives us hope that we may be able to cope better with some of our own past hurts. Even if we do not discuss them with our partner it feels as if they would not be shocked by them, because in some way they know about them. We hope that they will hold the solution to uncomfortable feelings of worthlessness in us and make us feel more whole or complete as a person. For whatever complex reasons, and whether we are conscious of them or not, there is an instinctive attraction to similar unmet emotional needs in our choice of partners.

Our parents' marriage also influences us. In discussion groups on marriage, I sometimes ask couples to reflect on their parents' relationships with each other, and think about what they admire and want to repeat, and what they want to avoid. The following are some of their remarks:

My father left too much decision making to my mother, and I want us to share more equally.

My father is quite tough, and I feel my mother doesn't stand up for herself enough. She doesn't seem to have a life of her own.

I was brought up by my mother, and I used to long for a dad at home. I don't want that for my kids.

Mum and Dad argue the whole time, and it wears everyone down. I can't stand it.

We also hear positive comments about parents who have been fun to be with, always welcoming to visitors, and so on. Sometimes the remarks are ambiguous:

My parents have a good relationship as far as I can tell, which presumably suits them. But we will work ours out differently—we're different people.

or

My parents' marriage seems ideal. They never seem to argue or row.

I must admit that last remark leaves me wondering about the equation of 'ideal' to 'not arguing', but that's another issue.

Some people cannot imagine their parents having sex. Some remember conflict over money. Others feel that their parents have set them standards which they would find difficult to reach in their own marriage. However, one thing is common to all couples and that is the presence of strong positive and negative feelings, which bear directly on their hopes and fears for their own marriage, and these, whether conscious or unconscious, have played their part in their choice of one another.

But why does this search go on inside us for some sort of replay of our family problems, when at a conscious level we

------

know very well what it is that we want to repeat or reject? We know that we are different personalities from either of our parents, even though we are the product of both. We do not feel the same inside as the parent who is of the same sex, or as the one whom we may resemble physically. Why is it that we so often find ourselves repeating the negative aspects of our family of origin? We cannot get away from the statistical evidence that negative family patterns repeat themselves. Children who are abused so often marry people who will abuse them. Workaholic fathers find they have workaholics sons and sons-in-law. Deprivation breeds deprivation, not inevitably, but often. Our conscious minds would tell us to marry as far away from our previous difficulties as we can, and yet subconscious influences at work inside us seem to say the opposite. What on earth is going on?

I described in Chapter 2 what a baby could gain from a parent about loving and being lovable: 'A sense of acceptance and of precious worth; ways of showing kindness and caring for another person; a sense of freedom to explore and experiment, to make mistakes and to tolerate their own and other people's limitations.' We might say the same about marriage, as this is the environment we need to continue growing as people. In our childhood all of this only happened to a limited extent. Other people's agendas took precedence over our own, and then we were left with our frustration, torn between our anger with others and the fear that it might have been our fault. We wondered if, perhaps, we were not particularly lovable, and we were to blame. Even the arrival of a new baby can make a child feel, 'What's wrong with me, that my parents should need another? Aren't I good enough for them?'

'Bad' feelings were also born out of the fact that we felt so much angrier and frustrated than we dared to express, so that we 'acted' loving when we didn't always feel it. Then, feeling a hypocrite, we despised ourselves for being so, and felt an inner lack of integrity.

Some deep sense of worthlessness is, I believe, common to us all, but we live in hope of proving to ourselves that this is not so. Marriage gives us a wonderful chance to rework the past, but in order to prove to ourselves that we are lovable, we have to set up similarities to the problems of childhood which threatened our identity then. Our hope is that this time round we can 'crack the problem' and prove ourselves to be lovable after all. But this part of our search for a partner is mostly subconscious. It has to do with the pain of being who we are, with our faults and failings, warts and all, and as these are thoughts we want to forget we manage to suppress them. In some marriages that pain is not allowed to surface. It feels too threatening to admit that we feel unlovable at times, or have doubts about our own worth. There is an unspoken agreement between the partners to live their marriage out on another level, in a way which feels 'good enough' and which does not rock the boat. In other marriages it surfaces horribly and the inner pain is seen as being caused by the partner. It then leads to a breakdown in the relationship and a repetition of the past.

A great number of couples do talk together about their own 'bad feelings'. They rework their past with each other's help — both the pain and the joy of it — as a normal part of the marriage journey. But we need to recognize the power of our subconscious and the fact that external pressures may cause it to erupt in strange ways. When this happens, some couples look to counsellors or therapists for help, and find that some of their feelings can be traced back to childhood or other experiences, and can be worked through and accepted. There are also times when a spiritual experience brings hidden feelings to the surface. Then, held in the safety of God's love, deep inner healing can take place.

There is a verse in Proverbs which reads, 'The purposes of a person's heart are deep waters, but a person of understanding draws them out.'[2] Sometimes that helper's talent is in the understanding of human relationships and sometimes it is in

---

the area of our relationship with God. These two wisdoms are not mutually exclusive but complimentary, a part of our growth towards loving God and our neighbours as ourselves.

In our choice of a partner, I have described a conscious and unconscious searching for someone similar to ourselves. There is also a longing for someone who will complement our personality, and make us feel more complete. We seem to be like 'nuts' looking for 'bolts' and vice versa! We seek out someone with a matching thread which runs right back through our past. Engineers call the nut and bolt 'male' and 'female' and the similarity to the genitals is obvious. In fact 'screwing' is one of the many slang terms for the sex act, but the conscious and unconscious 'fit' goes far deeper than a sexual match.

We all have married friends whose complementary personalities are obvious to us. The disorganized artist married to the tidy planner, the hot-tempered person married to a peace-maker, and so on. It is as if each is wanting to 'buy in' a part of themselves which they have been unable to own or develop and then together they will feel equipped to face the world.

The shy, sensitive person may need the courage of the person who is socially at ease, and can be the life and soul of the party. That other partner may be at times quite insensitive, treading on other people's toes, and need to have things pointed out by the shy partner.

In this complementary area of our pairings, an opportunity is created for each of us to grow, and maybe develop a side of our personality which did not develop in childhood. But it can have just the opposite effect, and mean that neither of us grows, because we rely entirely on our partner to provide the missing bits in ourselves. For example, Edith, who was frightened of saying anything confrontational, married Tom, who had a lot of suppressed anger in him, and who was quite happy to fight for both of them. Neither of them changed much throughout their fifty years of married life, and that was the way they both wanted it. This meant, though, that after Tom's death Edith was more bereaved and helpless than she might have been, had she learnt from Tom how to stand up for herself.

Our complementary qualities can also arouse envy or jealousy towards our partner. For example, the shy girl I mentioned will almost certainly be wishing that she could become more at ease socially. She may be expecting her husband to help her by providing a way in. He might begin to see her growing confidence as a threat. His inner voice may be saying, 'I don't want to share the limelight with her, I'm used to centre stage. That's the way I've been at home and school and I need it to stay that way.'

The mixture of conscious and unconscious elements in the choice of a partner beggars description. My husband remarked that it is like 'trying to get Einstein's theory of relativity on the back of an envelope'. All I can attempt to do is to give indications of some of the factors at work. But there is an instinct within us which chooses with surprising accuracy someone who is a match for us. In a committed partnership we each find someone to help us develop as a person, but for that growth to happen, each of us will be echoing something from each other's past which will uncover old hurts and challenge us again, and what a risky business that is. It could be so wonderful, or so awful, or as so often happens, it can be both on the same day.

In the bad moments the other person seems to be wrecking the vision of building together a shared life. It is then that we feel that this partner is the only person with whom we could feel so immobilized. They are not the best person for us, we feel, but the worst, because they touch so accurately our inner pains and hurts. And that is true. The Best and the Worst come together in one person, which takes us right back to our childhood fears, and the trapped feeling that comes with dependence. As children we wanted so much to be loved and found lovable. We found it intolerable to find the princess and the witch in one person, mother, and the prince and the ogre in the one father. Neither can we live comfortably with the good and bad feelings about ourselves; 'It's not my fault, it's yours', we say.

This incredible mixture of past and present, hopes and fears, good and bad, comes with us on the journey we call marriage. With us, too, comes the paradox that the best partner can become to us the worst, but also that the other person holds for us the possibility for a healing and growth which is tailor-made to each of our particular needs.

4

'Don't blame me!'

I wonder how often you have thought or said to your partner, 'If only you wouldn't . . .'

'If only you wouldn't interrupt me when I'm working.'

'If only you wouldn't do that when we are making love.'

'If only you wouldn't drive the car so fast.'

We could be describing any kind of habit that irritates us and we leave the sentence unfinished, because we all know how it ends. 'If only you would behave in the way that I behave then everyone would be happy'—or more accurately, 'I would be happy.' But of course our partner is feeling that anyone in their right mind would not fuss, and would see it their way.

Unless such remarks can be freed from their attacking nature and the defensiveness which they set up, they will either continue to irritate like a stone in the shoe, or develop into a row or a grudge. The 'If only' examples I have quoted above could be made by various people, in very different situations, but they get their true meaning from the histories of the couple who are using them in their own context.

The actual story behind the first remark is my own. Early in our married life my husband sometimes used to bring papers home from work and continue working on them after dinner, and it was he who said more than once, 'Do you have to interrupt me when I'm working!' When I was a child my mother worked from home as a fashion artist, and she employed someone to look after my brothers and me while she was in her studio. She locked the door to keep us from damaging her work or disturbing her concentration. No doubt we were a hazard. I still remember the day my three-year-old younger brother discovered her work table with a blue jug full of brushes and a pair of scissors and started to cut the tips off the brushes. When I wanted to see her, I would rattle the door handle and try to involve her in what I was doing. 'Go to Nurse' or 'Ask Nurse', she would say.

Thirty years later when my husband went upstairs to his study, I found myself having reasons to interrupt him. Perhaps I would take him a cup of coffee or remember a message to give him. Subconsciously, I did not like the feeling of his being unavailable. He found this quite irritating. His train of thought was broken, the message could have waited and he hadn't asked for the coffee. Usually he was patiently polite, but I picked up his irritation, which echoed my mother's same note of rejection. I repeat that I was not aware of any of this. My behaviour felt normal and caring, but it was actually motivated by an inner need to relieve feelings of discomfort.

A year or so later I heard someone describe an incident in her childhood about being locked in a cupboard. I suddenly saw myself rattling the studio door handle and felt the panic of the little girl inside me. Then my thoughts jumped to Paddy working at home, and in a moment of insight the connection was made. This insight gave me power over my feelings. They did not just go away, but I could help myself and separate the present reality from the past. Paddy had not known how accurate he had been in saying 'Do you *have* to interrupt me?' I had been responding to an inner compulsion to quieten a panic of which I was unaware.

Of course the present reality was still there. I was sometimes irritated that he was bringing his work home and I was wanting him to be involved in the affairs of the household. But because those emotions were still hooked into the little girl's panic inside me, they were carrying old hurt and anger which was finding an outlet in the present situation, and affecting my behaviour. When I was able to admit that, Paddy felt less guilty at having been impatient with me, and we were both more free to look at each other's needs as well as our own.

What was the gesture that upset the lover and made her say 'If only you wouldn't do that when we are making love'? It was a momentary smile that Gordon gave to Christine when they started to make love, and it felt to her like a leer from a dirty old man. Gordon never saw his parents touch each other in any show of affection, and his mother made no bones about sex being a 'dirty, messy business, unfortunately necessary for procreation, and one of God's bad bits of design'. No wonder Gordon felt slightly dirty every time he made love, even though he enjoyed it very much.

Christine's father had not actually interfered with her sexually when she was a little girl, but he had touched her up by letting his hands rove around inside her knickers as she sat on his knees, and this had made her feel invaded and insecure. She, too, enjoyed sex with Gordon, but was not quite free of a sense of being used, and Gordon's sheepish smile at being 'naughty' set off these feelings in her every time they made love.

Throw-away remarks often come from a deeper source than we realize, especially those we find ourselves repeating. Earlier I described marriage as a minefield, and both the previous examples show how we, like metal detectors, react not only to the obvious bits of metal on the ground, but sometimes buzz with a strength which indicates something much bigger under the ground. It may be explosive material or just an old tin can, but it's 'scary' to dig!

The third remark, 'If only you wouldn't drive so fast', could come out of any number of histories. It might arise out of fear from a past accident, awareness of a reckless streak in your partner, guilt from a previous row and knowing that your partner is relieving pent up feelings, or from some other thought. But while we express ourselves in a way which blames the other person, we are unlikely to find out what is really going on between us. Inevitably when a problem is seen as outside ourselves we lose contact with what is happening inside ourselves. On the other hand, suspending blame for ten minutes of our conversation can bring some surprising and important information to light.

Why are we so quick to blame others? And how did we develop this habit? To some extent we learnt it from our parents, but it is also part of a whole system of self-preservation which we constructed to protect and help us in our growing years. What we learnt from our parents and other teachers about blame varies a great deal. I saw an absurd example of this the other day when a mother was comforting her toddler. The two-year-old had just fallen over on the pathway and grazed its knee. The mother kissed the child, rubbed the knee and then hit the path with the palm of her hand, saying 'Naughty pavement!'

But I remember a more serious example of a couple who tried to protect their dearly loved and only child all through her growing years and into adulthood. Every failing she showed they projected on to other people in order to preserve her from pain, though in reality it was their own pain which they could not bear. The school didn't understand her, so they said, and the teacher was unfair, the school-friend was selfish, the first employer was too demanding, the second one was using her as a scapegoat, and so on. The girl felt unable to face the real world or herself as a real person. She felt a great pressure to live up to her parents' expectations and yet inside she was very aware of her failings. Because she had not been allowed to acknowledge them she became increasingly depressed and unable to cope.

Other parents blame their children frequently. Often one child in a family can feel that they are being picked on, receiving an unfair share of the blame. I mentioned earlier how children will take blame to themselves rather than question the goodness or reliability of the person on whom they depend: 'It must be me, I'm not the right sort of child for them', or 'I'm not worth their attention or affection.' Whether one is protected from blame or is blamed unfairly, or blames oneself, there is a large amount of inappropriate guilt mixed in with what might be appropriate, and this is an attack on the developing personhood of the child. It produces bad feelings which we have to 'dump' somewhere and any way of relieving them feels like salvation. It rescues us from inner pain when we can project the blame on to someone else, or on to the situation, on to our health or even on to the weather!

The way in which we protected our developing personhood through our growing years made sense in relation to that environment. But here we are in the adult world, unable to let go of those defences, using them in a random way and maybe expecting attack when none is intended. We may even do the attacking, as attacking is the first line of defence. And in marriage we have a partner who is ready-made to take our projections, a live-in scapegoat.

It is often said that we see in others what we most fear in ourselves, and one of our deepest fears is that we may indeed be like the 'bad' parent in our parents. If we deny it in ourselves and see it in our partner we will want to attack it there, because the threat is too near for comfort. I reckon that most of us do this at times.

Blaming others as a form of self-defence is only one method of self-protection. Perhaps the extent of our fear at being known, warts and all, can be measured by the very great lengths to which we go to stop people gaining an 'in-sight' into us. Of course the instinct for self-preservation is as strong as life itself and none of us would survive without some defence system in a real and raw world. We use it at work, in our family and in our friendships. But in marriage we are wanting a greater degree of trust and acceptance and closeness than we have experienced before, and this can only be achieved by a lowering of our defences.

It is risky to take off our armour and stand unprotected before someone we want to admire us. Do we trust their love enough to share our fears, or anger, or weaknesses with them, or do we feel that they will use our confessions in evidence against us at some later date?

A young man said to his wife in a counselling session, 'I know I switch off sometimes when you are talking to me, and I can see now that I'm doing what my father does to my mother.' It cost him a lot to admit that, but later on that week his wife became violently angry with him and said, 'You're so like your father, you know you are, you said so yourself!' She needed to hear from him, in another session, just how angry that remark had made him, how like his mother she had sounded, and how that was just why he had learnt to switch off. And she also needed to hear how she had traded on his openness of the previous week.

We may also defend ourselves from our own critical or hostile feelings towards our partner by idealizing them. We put them on a pedestal where they will be safe from harm. 'I think the world of my husband, he's done so well, and he's so good to me.' But this was not the whole story. As it unfolded she had considerable envy of his success and there was pain at the loss of what might have been her own career.

We often deny our feelings. 'No, I'm not cross. I'm perfectly prepared to listen.' We have used the right words, but our partner knows from the tone in our voice that it is just not true. Or we can defend ourselves from criticism by taking all the blame and turning our anger against ourselves. 'It's all my fault. I'm a useless sort of person. I don't know why you stay with me.' This is also a discussion stopper and a change of agenda.

We can have a row with the boss, come home and slam the door, kick the cat, take it out on the children and set up a chain reaction round the family. We can get obsessive about tidiness or timekeeping or whatever, in a desire to control the outside world and so protect ourselves from our inner world of uncontrollable feelings.

We can deny our sexual feelings with high or holy talk. We can intellectualize a problem to cover up its emotional content, or generalize about life in a detached philosophical way. We can make a joke when the conversation touches us closely, or change the subject. We have got so used to our own methods that we hardly recognize that we are defending ourselves, but often our partner knows, and their pointing it out will be likely to drive us into defending ourselves even more fiercely. Unfortunately, the problem we create in our marriage by not facing a difficult situation between us can be greater than the one we are trying to avoid.

It is not that every irritation between a couple needs attention. In any marriage there has to be give and take, and 'live and let live'. We can accept each other's moods and foibles to some extent because we love our partner and we know that we too have our off-days and our personal traits. But we also know that certain subjects are almost guaranteed to produce an argument. My son at twenty-four years remarked from the back of the car, 'Oh shut up, you two. You are always arguing about the route you take.' Neither of us had realized what an observable habit we had developed, or what an uncomfortable atmosphere we were creating. But this is a trivial example in comparison with the areas of conflict which we are afraid might cause a real explosion between us and injure us. Yet the longer these are left, the more likelihood there is of damage. It may be that of being blown apart or drifting apart, or of going on together in a paralysed fashion with no-go areas, but either way we suffer pain and loss.

I hope that what I have said so far indicates that neither partner ever has enough information about the other person's inner world to make quick value judgements on them. So, early in a conflict situation, we need to ask for and give each other more information so that we may understand better.

The process I am describing is set out in a chart on the next page. This is often referred to as the 'Pinch/Crunch' chart[1]. It shows the various stages in the development of a relationship between two people.

When a couple meet, each brings with them their own assumptions about life and relationships. They also bring their particular needs and fears and their individual talents. Then they share information about themselves and their expectations, and find out whether they can give and take and develop a closer relationship. If they cannot, one or other of them will leave, but if they fit well together they will clarify their roles and their commitment to one another as they chat about the future. What commitment means for a couple and whether or not marriage is seen as the sealing of that varies very much in today's society, but they will reach what they consider a stable relationship.

The chart then identifies two stages of eruption for conflicts between them. The 'Pinch' is the stage when a problem comes to light with sufficient clarity to be an issue. If it is not addressed, there will be an inevitable build-up of resentment and anger, which will affect the way in which one or both partners see themselves and each other. They may feel ambiguous and uncertain about their role in the marriage. Feelings run high, and the choices seem more stark. Then comes the 'Crunch' point, 'We can't go on like this, something has to change.'

When the 'fit' between the partners starts to pinch there are three options: to negotiate it openly, or in a more covert way, or to ignore it. We all negotiate indirectly with our partners. At times we might buy flowers, be reluctant in sex, or do whatever we feel makes our point without words. This kind of

---

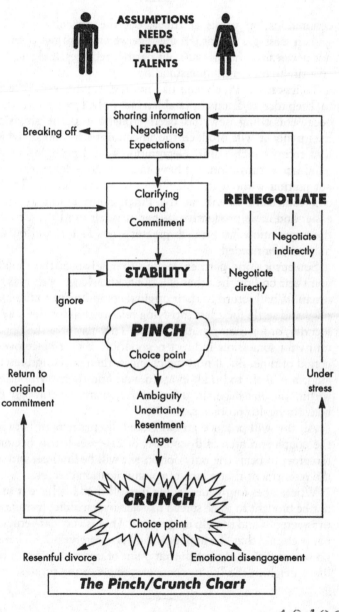

The Pinch/Crunch Chart

18429

communication works at times, but the difficulty with unspoken messages is that the message we are wanting to send is not necessarily the message our partner receives, and that can give rise to more misunderstanding.

To ignore the Pinch feels like not rocking the boat. It seems to keep the relationship stable, but only for a short time, because nothing new has been brought into the situation. Eventually it will produce the uncertainty and anger which lead to a Crunch point. Negotiation is still possible but the build-up of frustration will have made it more difficult to hear our partner without the blaming process taking over. To discuss something openly at the Pinch point is usually much easier and more productive. When it is left until the Crunch, the negotiation has a much greater stress factor, and outside help may be needed.

Sometimes one partner, feeling themselves at the Crunch point and finding the other will not acknowledge or discuss the situation, will return to their original commitment to the marriage and settle for a less satisfying relationship for the sake of security, or for their children's sake. This may give the opportunity for some slow indirect negotiation to take place over a period of time. But if nothing changes, then anger and resentment are likely to build up again, and find their own outlets, within the marriage, in difficulties at work, or through the body, in health problems.

All this will produce an emotional disengagement between the couple; an area of discomfort or dis-ease. If this becomes too great to bear, the only option left will be divorce, with all the resentment that a lack of communication creates.

Where does forgiveness come into all this? I believe it must not be brought in to be spread like jam over a difficult situation to sweeten it and to help us ignore it. That is very dangerous. It has been said that 'To understand all is to forgive all.'[2] There is no way any of us can reach that point of understanding in this life, though in the life to come we are given the promise that 'then we shall fully know, even as we are fully known' (by God alone).[3] However, when we are prepared to be open with one another and to give each other more information about our inner thoughts and feelings, this usually improves our understanding and makes us slower to blame, as in the examples given at the beginning of the chapter. Of course, increased insight into our own behaviour will also have a transforming effect.

The need to forgive those we love and the longing to be forgiven have been with us since childhood. There each family had its own rules. We learnt how much forgiveness we could expect and for what 'sins'. But all of us have a residue of guilty and angry feelings from our past. It is at this point that I find the Lord's Prayer so profound: '. . . forgive us our trespasses as we forgive those who trespass against us.'[4] When we think of our sinfulness before God, we touch feelings of real and imagined guilt, and of anger which has sometimes been appropriate and at other times not so. We also touch feelings of our own worthlessness which are not from God. This prayer recognizes that the origin of many of these feelings comes from the fact that we were first trespassed against. The use of the word 'sin' in our modern translation is much too general a word for me. Trespass — walking over someone else's property and not respecting their rights — pictures very accurately the way in which we all trample over one another's sensitive or private areas and do not respect another's personality. We use and abuse one another, both intentionally and unintentionally, and it is as a defenceless baby that we first experience this.

What Christ verbalized in the prayer was our common need to become aware that we have been trespassed against, as well as our need to recognize what we do to others. The little child in us has been wounded, and in anger and self-defence is wanting to wound back. It is not easy to forgive those who hurt us. But if this vicious circle of damage which we call 'the fall' is to be broken, then somehow love has to be reborn in us. For me the belief that God knows about and understands my feelings of hurt and loves me as I am gives me a sense of acceptance and inner warmth. My personality is valued and I can believe that I have worth. This makes it more possible for me to admit that I also hurt other people, even if I am not always aware of it. And I have to allow that they too may not always be very self-aware.

Remembering that I have been 'trespassed against' highlights my hurts and makes me aware that forgiveness is costly. It calls forth a love for that other person of the same degree as I wish for myself in their shoes. In other words it requires that I show mercy in order to be able to receive it, and the little word 'as', in the phrase 'forgive . . . as we forgive', affirms that there is a continuous process being described here of being forgiven and forgiving. Christ's desire to heal me through giving me back a proper self-worth is part of the essence of his gift to me, enabling me to give and receive more forgiveness with my fellow human beings.

It is costly for him to accept us just as we are, but in our bones we know that a forgiving love has to be costly for it to be real. His love and understanding reach back to the damage done to my personhood from birth onwards and as I have become aware of that love having been there for me, before any response was expected, it feels appropriate to speak of a moment of new awareness as 'being born again' — of the Spirit. Unlike our physical birth, this can happen again and again. Little pieces of our damaged spirit are given new life, but the healing process will not be completed in this life, even though the Spirit of Christ within can grow in us day by day.

And so, as we ponder our own need to forgive and be forgiven, I believe that we become more self-aware and sensitive to others. This inevitably affects our understanding of love and of conflict. Even so, our insights into both will always be very limited in this life.

5

Closeness and separateness

Central to the marriage relationship is the finding of a comfortable movement for both partners between a developing sense of togetherness and a respect for each other's personal space. The best and worst of marriage are exposed in this struggle.

Poets capture some of the yearnings and wounds involved. This example expresses something of the hope for togetherness:

> I would I could adopt your will,
> See with your eyes, and set my heart
> Beating by yours, and drink my fill
> At your soul's springs,—your part, my part
> In life, for good and ill.
>
> Robert Browning[1]

and this the despair:

> *What is a marriage of two?*
> The loss of one
> By wounds or abdication; a true
> Surrender mocked, an unwished victory won:
> Rose, desert — mirage too.
>
> C. Day Lewis[2]

The sense of bliss in unity:

———

I wonder by my troth, what thou, and I
Did, till we lov'd? . . .

My face in thine eye, thine in mine appears
And true plaine hearts do in the faces rest
                                    John Donne[3]

and the pretence:

> Call it a good marriage:
> They never fought in public,
> They acted circumspectly
> and faced the world with pride;
> Thus the hazards of their love-bed
> were none of our damned business —
> Till as jurymen we sat upon
> Two deaths by suicide.
>   Robert Graves[4]

The contentment:

At the sea-end of the town, Mr and Mrs Floyd, the cocklers,
are sleeping as quiet as death, side by wrinkled side, tooth-
less, salt and brown, like two old kippers in a box.
                                    Dylan Thomas[5]

and the process:

Love one another, but make not a bond of love:
Let it rather be a moving sea between the shores of your
souls.
. . .
Sing and dance together and be joyous, but let each one
of you be alone,
Even as the strings of a lute are alone though they quiver
with the same music.
                                    Kahlil Gibran[6]

———

As I read these verses I feel almost overwhelmed by the range and intensity of the feelings they express, and I know too that they can all be felt within one marriage. As a child I was fascinated by magnets. I wondered why it was that two pieces of metal when placed together one way round should stick so closely that I could hardly pull them apart, and when I turned one or other of them round I could not bring them together however hard I tried. I would begin to move them towards each other, but then something inside the metal took over and they actively pushed each other away. I have often heard these push/pull feelings described by married couples.

Couple 1

I take a week's sailing each year and I reckon I need it. Surely it's not too much to ask to spend time with old friends and get some real exercise. But every time it comes up she moans. I can see it coming. She really resents my sailing friends, even if I just have a drink with one of them after work. It's as if she thinks they are trying to break up our marriage. It's ridiculous!

Couple 2

I like it when Jenny and I can relax together and watch TV, but she is usually busying herself with something and she won't just come and sit down beside me. There will always be things waiting to be done, but I think that they are not always as important as 'us'.

Couple 3

I come up to bed reasonably early, thinking how much I would like to have a cuddle and make love and I usually say, 'Don't be too long, will you?' And then I wait . . . and wait . . . and by the time he comes up I've fallen asleep, or am too drowsy to want to be aroused. Then he says I never want sex, and I'm always too tired. Whose fault is that!

Couple 4

He said he wanted us to be closer, but what happened? We planned a holiday together, and then he asked another couple to join us. Yes, I like them too, but we need time together and it is hard to get that because of the demanding nature of our separate jobs. Then just when we get a golden opportunity, he messes it up.

Couple 5

He comes with me to choose my clothes, drives me to visit friends, and then wants me to tell him what conversations we had. The worst of it is that he wouldn't let me take a job. He says he can support me and he won't have the neighbours thinking otherwise. Well, I did get a job last month, helping with school lunches. I love it, but of course I'm home by the time he gets back so he can't complain.

These extracts of conversations are cries for closeness and cries for separateness. In each case the speaker is both blaming the partner and feeling misunderstood. It is worth noting that the issue is not about the problem described because some couples always holiday with friends and some wives never seem to sit down in the evening. In some marriages the couple find other times to make love when neither is too tired. Some partners take separate holidays on occasions and some wives love their husbands to come shopping for clothes and do not want to have a job. But these particular partners are describing great discomfort, and in order to find out why, we need to see if there is a connection with their past experiences of closeness and separateness.

The man who wanted a week's sailing had grown up with a very demanding and ailing mother. He was a good boy at home, but he had to be at his mother's beck and call and this was quite a burden to him. There were times when he would rather be out with his friends on their bikes. Inside him was a build-up of resentment of having been deprived of fun and not given enough time with his peer friendships. Now he saw his wife in his mother's role, demanding, and spoiling his fun. In this frame of mind he could not see her as a person in her own right. He felt too persecuted inside. Nor did she know how powerful in him was the fear of a woman's ability to spoil his fun.

The girl who never sat down was someone who needed to keep things well under control. She was an illegitimate child whose early years had been spent between various relatives. Inside she felt a mess, but outside she kept herself and her home beautifully. She had such a low opinion of herself that she could not believe it would be of value to her husband for her to sit down beside him for fifteen minutes. She needed to prove her worth in what she did for the family in a way that they or she could see. The very thing she needed, which was to be valued for herself as a person, was the very thing she could not take, because it would put her in touch with those old feelings of worthlessness.

The couple who did not go to bed at the same time were both uneasy about taking sexual initiative. She made out that she was available, but did not actually say anything like 'Let's have some fun in bed tonight. Do come up soon.' He got the mixed message very accurately and played out his own am-bivalence by coming up later. Each could blame the other without acknowledging their own part in it.

The young man who asked the couple to share their holiday was afraid of what might be expected of him if they were alone. He felt his wife wanted a greater display of affection than he had in him to give. She had often said as much, so how could he cope with fourteen whole days together? When he was eighteen months old his mother had had a little girl whose health was poor from birth, and he had felt that he must fend for himself. Later on he was sent to boarding-school. No one in his family was demonstrative in their affection and he grew up as a loner. He very much wanted it to be otherwise and he had learned how to survive in a group both at school and in the local youth club. He could feel a degree of warmth and sociability in the group, but closer than that felt too close for comfort. Instinctively he had turned their holiday into a group activity.

The couple who went shopping for clothes together both came from hard and deprived backgrounds, and had clung to each other for survival. But now the wife was trying to find her own identity through a little more separateness, which was making her husband feel unwanted again, an echo from his childhood.

As we explored in Chapter 2, both closeness and separateness arouse ambivalent sets of feelings which were created in our growing years. To be close to a parent could mean being safe and accepted, even blissful, in an atmosphere in which to blossom and grow, or it could mean being limited and dominated and feeling trapped. To be separate from a parent could feel like freedom to grow and develop as an individual, or like rejection, abandonment, and panic. Closeness may have meant suppressing our own needs and feelings, and pretending to be different on the outside from our true inner self. No wonder then that as adults we find it risky to say what we actually think.

Closeness to a parent may have meant being a parent to one's own parent. Many people find that their own children's love for them makes up to them for what they did not experience themselves as children. It makes them very dependent on their children for their own well-being, and the child picks this up. It is a heavy burden for the child to carry, but because it needs to preserve its security it will often do the best it can. Sometimes the child will become anxious about the parent and act in a very caring way. In doing so it earns the response of the parent's gratitude and love. This feels a good reward but there is still a buried resentment at having been robbed of a carefree childhood and 'put upon'. It is not difficult to see how marriage can reactivate these feelings, as soon as one or other partner wants to be cared for, and how this can get tangled up with issues over closeness and separateness.

To find the hidden meaning behind the sort of tensions I have described, we have to explore the feelings they arouse and communicate them to our partners. Two very relevant questions to ask ourselves are, 'Have I ever felt this way before?', and 'Is there any similarity between this situation and anything in my past?'

It is often said that men find it harder to be in touch with their feelings and to express them than women. I would say both yes and no to this. It is true that social training makes it harder for a man to show 'weakness'. 'Big boys don't cry' is embedded in British culture. It has also been demonstrated in videoed experiments that little boys play with toys differently from little girls. For the boys the game or toy is the focus and they relate with other boys towards that objective goal, while the girls often use the game or toy as a connection through which to form relationships with the other children. But I feel a resistance to stereotyping here, because I often find that once a husband is given permission to own his feelings and express them, he is just as competent at it as his wife, sometimes more so. Maybe this is because it can bring him the relief and release of a new-found freedom.

But what about the difficulty of having a close time together to discuss an area of concern when closeness and separateness is the issue. Here the problem itself is often acted out. The one who wants more closeness moves towards the partner in wanting to talk about it, only to see the partner edge away, change the subject, or go out.

Early in our marriage, my husband and I found ourselves behaving in this way. I felt he was running away from discussing matters to do with ourselves and our children, and he felt I was making mountains out of molehills. On the advice of a wise psychotherapist friend we set up a time each week for talking together about personal things which were on our mind, or practical difficulties in the family. The bargain was that I would save the matters I wanted us to discuss until that occasion, and Paddy would set the time aside for nothing else. It seemed unnatural to relate in such a structured way, and I had to stop myself several times during the week from 'going on about things', and save them until Thursday. Paddy on the other hand found himself getting anxious as Thursday drew near. He remarked that he could feel his stomach getting tighter.

At our first 'appointment' we tried to be as open as possible and as confronting as necessary. We covered several matters and in the process we both discovered that our private fears — mine of never being heard and his of being swamped — were largely unfounded. Even though we held some different opinions we were much more able to listen to one another than we had expected. When the session came to a natural end, we found that it had only taken us an hour, though when we set it up we had promised to spend as long as it took. Not every Thursday session was smooth but we continued with this arrangement for about two months. Then we let the enforced Thursday structure go, because it seemed that we had broken a vicious circle of fear and could choose our times more naturally.

During these two months we identified an important factor in our way of relating. This was our tendency to polarize. To give an example, I had been growing concerned over several weeks about the behaviour which one of our children was exhibiting, and I was not sure how to deal with it. I wanted to chew it over with Paddy, and think aloud with him, but he felt that he was expected to find a solution, and felt helpless to do so. He had assumed that I, as a mother, would instinctively know how to cope. The thought that I might not cope made him anxious, so he kept reassuring me that I was managing

———

very well. I felt he was not listening to my fears and so I repeated them more strongly. 'I'm worried' changed to 'I'm very worried', and he reassured me more vehemently. He began to say that I was getting things out of proportion, and I would reply that he either didn't care or was blind. We had started from a shared concern for the children, but in our anxiety we were pushing each other further and further away. When we saw the 'game' we were unconsciously playing, it made it possible for us to listen differently. Again and again we found that the break in communication came for us at the point where our individual fears met, as it did in this case.

Roger and Donna Vann, in their book *Secrets of a Growing Marriage*,[7] recommend couples to have a marriage retreat two or three times a year. The couple are advised to go away together for a day or a weekend, having made an agenda and a timetable the week before, which they then work through. It is not a holiday but a working time together. They also recommend an evening a week having a quiet meal together for mutual enjoyment. In most families this takes some forward planning!

The lifestyle which many of us lead today requires us to structure and monitor our time very closely. It may be that our marriage 'servicing' needs to go into the diary along with the car service, or it will get squeezed out of existence. In fact some of us take more initiative over booking our cars in or planning a day to service them ourselves than we do over maintaining our marriage relationship. Of course it does take more courage to inspect the component parts of our shared life, but, like the car, the longer we leave it the more likely it is to let us down, perhaps when we least expect it.

Several organizations run marriage growth weekends, and some people find it helpful when a programme is imposed on them from outside. Others have a close relationship with one other couple with whom they can be very honest and open, and they meet with them for mutual support on a regular basis.

———

What each of us needs is a way to communicate at the 'Pinch' place which works for us, so that we do not fall into the trap of believing that if we ignore it, it will go away.

Tensions over closeness and separateness can be played out in any area of our marriage, but sometimes the very sight of the double bed reminds us of all that we long for and do not seem to be achieving. Lying side by side, we behave like the magnets I mentioned before. We are either drawn together and unite our bodies, or even just hold hands before we drop off to sleep, or we recoil from the physical closeness which only exaggerates the emotional gap between us. Unresolved quarrels can have a real 'turn off' effect on our sex life.

A partner will sometimes describe this by saying that they no longer fancy their partner sexually and that this has driven them apart emotionally. He or she has fallen out of love. The chemistry between them has altered and there is no future for them together. In my experience it is much more likely to happen in the reverse order. It is the emotional conflict which is driving them apart, and this is borne out by the way in which their sex life can revive when the real problems are discovered and discussed.

There are times when our need for separateness is nothing to do with our partner. We may love them dearly, but be needing space in which to get back inside our own skin. It may be that we are suffering from overwork or overexposure to people and problems, and closeness to anyone just feels like a demand. Our partner may feel rejected because they are not being given the chance to make us feel better through closeness.

I have known couples when this kind of need could not be recognized. In one case a husband, who had a very responsible job, sometimes had business meetings which lasted well into the evening. He then had an hour's drive back home. It seemed to his wife that within minutes of arriving home he would set up a quarrel and stride out of the room. He would then sleep in the spare room. The following breakfast would start with an argument about who was to blame for their sleeping in separate rooms.

If the husband had been able to communicate his need to his wife, and explain to her what the day had done to him, she would have had the chance to give him extra space. But in the event, he was projecting his uncomfortable feelings on to her, and seeing her as 'that wretched woman who insists on being close when I need to be alone.' When his wife realized his need to be alone she said to him, 'You don't need to force a quarrel to sleep in the spare room. Sometimes it's nice to sleep alone.' She told me later that this led to a relaxed pattern in which either could choose a solitary night without feeling that it was the beginning of the end, but this was only after they had had several years of hurt and misunderstanding.

Allowing each other space requires a real respect for the other person's different needs and a trust in their returning. For some people this is much more threatening than for others, especially for those who once gave their trust to someone who went away and did not return.

How close is close enough? Obviously the answer will always be intensely personal to each couple, but it has to do with a willingness in both partners to break new ground inside themselves. I see marriage as a dance between two people, which they invent together and develop as they go along. It involves risk, as the initiative moves backwards and forwards between them and as each pulls the other closer or steps back from them. For both it is a venture into the unknown in which each will have to give up the safety of their own known way and to some extent lose control. These moments are like little deaths, which have to be experienced before the possibility of the next new part of their life together can be discovered.

The similarity to the way of the cross is striking. Christ both enacts and teaches a way of life. He uses different metaphors to describe it, one being in the death of the seed to bring forth fruit. This way of life is written right through creation as an inescapable truth; that new life requires the death of the old and known.

What does it mean to be together as one flesh and yet to remain separate personalities? Robin Skynner describes the sex act as one in which each person needs the other to be most fully themselves. I do not believe that we are meant to submerge our identity under the influence of another, or to so fuse it with another that its boundary is lost. The church has sometimes overstressed 'oneness' in marriage at the expense of the woman's personality, but I do not see this in the teaching or behaviour of Christ towards women. The process of dying to self has to be a choice, taken in the faith that somehow we shall be more complete by doing so.

The doctrine of the Trinity describes God as one person in three persons, and three in one. It is not about three persons who are each a 'third of a person'. John Donne's meditation 'No man is an Island'[8] also wrestles with the mystery that each of us is more than ourselves in isolation. Something about us does not exist except in relationship, in communion, in community. We need other people to be most fully ourselves.

My husband and I and our children lived for five years in a Christian community. Here we saw very clearly that those who were most able to be a part of the community were those who were able to be alone with themselves. Separateness is food for togetherness and vice versa. But in Christian communities fantasies abound about what it 'ought' to be like, and they can be very destructive to the life. I would like to rephrase here a quote from Dietrich Bonhoeffer about community life,[9] and relate it to married life.

> He who loves his dream of marriage more than the marriage itself becomes a destroyer of the latter, even though his personal intentions may be ever so honest and earnest and sacrificing.

6

Loving and losing

My mother used to quote from Tennyson, the Victorian Poet Laureate,

> 'Tis better to have loved and lost
> Than never to have loved at all.[1]

I still believe that, but I have become more aware that an experience of loving and losing can be so painful that it may stop us giving our affection wholeheartedly on the next occasion.

I have also realized that we cannot take hold of a new situation properly until the previous one is put down and allowed to go. There is a process to be experienced, a proper ending before a good beginning. The placenta and its umbilical cord is cut from the baby when it enters this world. It belonged to the world of the womb, and it cannot be dragged around with us here. It is not just in the dance we invent together in marriage that we need to let go of the old to experience the new, but at every stage in life.

People come into marriage with very different experiences of loss. Some of us may have gone through childhood and the teens without ever having experienced the death of anyone close to us. We may have found the transitions from home to school and then to the big wide world smooth and exciting. We had grown out of the old situation and we welcomed the new with open arms. We did not feel that we had lost security or love and had had a struggle to find it again because the time had been right. We were ready to let go and grow into the new situation. But others of us have experienced traumas of loss which have left their mark on us. We are often taught to discount these traumas in ourselves, even though it takes courage to put our feelings behind us and get on with life.

'Other people have it worse' is a common attitude of grown-ups to children who appear to be wallowing in self-pity and we may have been taught to push our feelings underneath before they have been properly experienced and valued. In fact, those who wallow are often those whose pain has not been recognized and given worth by others at the time, so that they are left with their muddled feelings of loss, having all the more reason to hold on to them because no one else seems to care.

As well as personal losses, there are universal ones experienced by us all. These are losses of freedom and control, of security and love, of privacy and respect, which we experience as a normal part of growing up in a world peopled by others like us, who fight for survival and identity in the jungle of life. Our immediate felt needs at any one time may conflict with the needs of the group, whether at home or school or in society, and we have to give in, 'lose face' or 'lose out' in that situation. As I mentioned in Chapter 4, we will have found ways of defending ourselves against the pain of these experiences, but events in later life may awaken an old pain, without reviving the memory of where it began, and we find ourselves in the grip of irrational fears or dreams.

A girl, aged twenty-seven, came in for counselling one day in an acutely depressed state. This was her first visit. She said that she had even thought of suicide during the past month. The reason she gave was that her boyfriend had left her after a relationship of about four months. She went into great detail about how awful this was for her. Somehow her reactions to this event seemed out of proportion, but as we began to explore her story it came to light that she had had a previous boy/girl relationship from her school days which had lasted seven years. She had expected that it would lead to marriage after her college course, but at twenty-two, during her last term, her boy-friend had suddenly left her for someone else. During the same week her father told her that her mother had terminal cancer. She was very near finals and her father urged her to go through with the exams, knowing how important they would be for her future career. She did so, making every effort to push the shock and grief out of her mind and concentrate on her work. She passed her finals, and then her mother died at the same time as the start of her first job. Again she had to push down her grief to cope with the new situation at work. She had never found the opportunity to let herself feel the emotions of those traumatic events and give to herself the space to grieve. She needed to feel again the desolation and the loss, to express her great anger, and to talk and talk about what those two people had meant to her. The recent affair was as nothing in comparison with these past emotions, and by being helped to get in touch with them she began to be able to separate the past from the present and see the present in a truer light.

My husband lost one of his brothers in a climbing accident many years ago. At the time he maintained a stiff upper lip, though they had been very close. He did not make a conscious choice to do so, but he had learnt from childhood that this was the accepted way to deal with sadness and grief. Years later when our dog had to be 'put down', he suddenly found himself in floods of tears. He felt that in some way his grief was inappropriate, carrying something more. He knew that he had loved the dog, but his love for his brother had been infinitely greater and deeper. And then a host of memories of his brother came flooding back and he began to feel the sadness of that loss.

A friend confided in me recently that her father had died when she was fourteen years old. At twenty she entered into an unworkable marriage which ended in divorce after two years, leaving her with a great sense of failure. Later on she married again, and now has a loving, stable relationship in which she has been able to get back a lot of her self-worth.

———

Even so, if she and her husband have a disagreement, she finds herself dreaming at night that he is leaving her. Those past losses still resonate with unresolved pain and guilt in the subconscious mind.

Grieving is a process, and if we have some understanding of it, we can be more help to each other in weathering the losses we will experience during our life. It will also help us to recognize the source of our own feelings. When we lose a person who has been very important to us, at first we can hardly believe that they are no longer here. We may experience a certain numbness of feeling. People often find themselves arranging the funeral with a coolness which makes them feel quite guilty, though it seems to me that nature is being kind in giving us our feelings of loss slowly, so that we can handle them more easily. We can sometimes find ourselves searching for the person. I remember a friend telling me that she had lost her father when she was nine years old and she used to look at the crowds in the street for a long time after with some sort of faint hope that he might reappear.

Then we yearn for the dead person and we become angry with them for leaving us. Didn't they realize how important they were to us? We may be angry with God for allowing it to happen, and angry with ourselves for not having said or done certain things, or for having behaved towards them in a way we now regret. We may blame ourselves for having contributed in some way to their pain. Our anger and guilt can be very strong and at the same time very hard to acknowledge. And so it takes up residence in the subconscious and the suppressed energy of it comes out in depression.

In the grieving process it is our anger which we are most likely to deny. We then project the anger somewhere else, often on to those who are nearest to us. We can take hold of a minor irritation with our partner and inflate it like a balloon, so that it contains sufficient angry energy and 'puff' to relieve the pressure of our internal discomfort for the time being. They tell us that

———

we are being unreasonable, and rightly so, because the reasons are mainly unconnected to the present irritation. It can help a great deal to sit with our feelings and try to recognize our anger. If we can also talk about it, with someone we trust to listen and not to help us deny it, that is even more help.

If the grieving process continues healthily, meaning 'towards our wholeness', then it will gradually move us towards our being able to let the dead person go. This is not about forgetting them, but about experiencing a change within us which frees us to take to ourself some of the qualities which we have experienced as a part of them. A simple example of this would be of a wife who takes on the garden after her husband dies and, though she did not show much interest in it previously, she now takes to herself the interest and expertise which belonged to her husband. St John of Chrystostom, a fourth-century archbishop, wrote 'He whom we love and lose is no longer where he was before. He is now wherever we are.' This is the completed process through which we become enriched by our past relationships.

But as I have said, present losses can echo past losses. Unfortunately, the greater the losses we have had in our past and the younger we were, the more we will have suppressed in order to protect ourselves from the desolation and anger which felt too great to bear. Therefore we will be less likely to enter into a present loss and allow the process to have its way in us.

When we marry, each partner will have learnt to face loss differently, and so we may make some very inaccurate judgements about one another. One of my daughters told me many years after my father's death — which happened when she was ten — that she did not think that I could have minded very much because she never saw me cry. It was a natural deduction for her to make, but little could she realize how confused my feelings had been, and what a mixture of anger and love, fear and respect had been paralysing my emotions at the time. It took me several years to acknowledge those feelings.

Some couples have to face tragic losses in their life. I do not believe that any of us can pass judgement on a couple who have found that the pain and stress of the trauma has broken their relationship. The loss of health, of a limb, or the loss of a child can be so hard to bear that we need a great deal of support. But we can be some help to one another just by valuing each other's pain and letting our partner know that we do so. We can also help by not trying to hurry the grieving process, and by being a little more tolerant with one another's irrational moments of anger, not taking them too personally. We may even be able to help one another to make connections with past losses which may be relevant.

But we cannot always help each other. One such occasion might be when a husband or wife has been married before and has lost their former partner by death or divorce. Someone outside the situation, in a caring professional capacity, can often help to identify unresolved feelings about the loss. This can save the new relationship from becoming the container for emotions which belong elsewhere. Second marriages have a higher rate of breakdown, and this is partly due to the difficulty of recognizing the past feelings and of being able to let the past go before moving into the new situation.

I have gone into some detail about loss because life is a process of continual change and every gain means some kind of a letting go. The loss of singleness is the first one we experience as a result of gaining a partner. It was nice, we remember, when we did not have to let someone else know our movements, and ring when we were going to be late. And we could spend money on ourselves more easily. Most of the time we reckon that the gains of married life far outweigh the losses, but sometimes a partner behaves as though they ought to be able to 'have their cake and eat it'.

Redundancy, unemployment and even retirement may bring a loss of status and a loss of the image we had of ourselves. We lose a role, an income, our activity and interest, maybe our self-esteem. Loss of our youth through the natural ageing process means a gradual facing of our mortality. We shall not be here for ever. I can remember at least two men speaking to me about their panic at growing old. They both felt that it made them fanatical about keeping fit and doing sport, and in both cases this was affecting their marriage.

For women, the menopause brings the end of being able to bear children. Many women go through great grief at this. Some feel they have lost their sexuality and they must therefore be less attractive to men. Some have to face the certainty of childlessness, others sudenly just feel older. The menopause can take a few years and any low self-esteem can be increased by times of feeling physically unwell. Some stop making any effort to look after their appearance and actually appear less attractive.

All this can be happening at a time when the husband is having to recognize that he has reached the peak of his career, or is in sight of it. He can no longer live with the hope of greater things for himself. He too is needing affirmation of worth from his wife, just as she is from him. There may be nearly-adult children in the family whose virility, attractiveness, and energy sharpen the parents' sense of their own loss. It is not surprising if the marriage relationship is stressed by all this and, sadly, it is often after about twenty years of marriage that one or other partner looks outside the marriage for the fulfilment of their need to be valued.

Learning to recognize feelings of loss is a very important part of becoming a mature adult. It also makes us face the facts and let go of the fantasies. It makes us more self-aware and more sensitive to those around us. My two-year-old grandson was in tears today because he had grown out of his shoes and had to wear a new stiff pair that didn't feel nearly as comfortable. No amount of sensible reasoning would help; the process of learning to cope with loss starts very young!

7

Sex and gender

Fact and fantasy could be the title for a book on sex alone. Not only can our imagination clash with reality, but we can also feed our imagination with erotic mental images to gratify sexual desires. In looking at the sexual side of our relationship, we can touch on some of our very best moments together, and some of our worst. Again, in order to understand the present we need to go back to the past, and look at the ideas and feelings we brought with us from the whole of our life experience before we met each other.

We come into the world as one of a kind. We are either male or female. We also contain something of that 'other kind', because we all have both male and female hormones, though the ratio is different. We have grown up with varying degrees of contact and closeness to the opposite sex, but we can never be 'of their kind'. We therefore live in a tension between having some perception of what it feels like to be a member of the opposite sex, and yet never being able to know from the inside. There is a natural fear of the unknown in us all, which gives rise to a desire to control it, lest it control us, and nowhere is the battle for control more obviously played out than between the sexes.

We also have an innate fear of abandonment and a desire to complete ourselves in an intimate relationship with a man/ woman who will make us feel more fully ourselves.

All this — the fear of the unknowable, the desire to control, the fear of loneliness and the need for the other kind to complete us — makes male/female relationships both very risky and at the same time the most exciting and satisfying.

_____

What is your gender, male or female? And how has that affected how you see yourself as a person? What messages, spoken or unspoken, did your family give you about what it meant to be one of your gender? What do you think were your parents' assumptions of how their world expected them to be? How was a woman to be a woman, and a man to be a man? Were there expectations about clothing, or manners, or role which were given to you?

It can be an illuminating exercise to mark out a sheet of paper in decades, and think back into what it felt like to be you at each stage in your life. Thinking first of the period from birth to ten years old, when can you first remember realizing you were a little boy or a little girl? Remember the incident. Did it feel good or not, and who was it made you feel that way? Or do you remember feelings of great uncertainty about your gender? What other incidents can you remember, and what influenced you from home, school, church teaching, and peer group pressure? And what notions and feelings did you collect about the opposite sex? Jot down what comes to mind, and continue with these questions through each decade of your life.

And what do you remember about your early ideas of sexuality and the sex act? What fantasies did you catch from those around you, and what were you told? Would you have thought it was fun, naughty, dirty, secret, the way babies are made, or what? It is worth spending some time on this, because it is out of this material that each of us has built our earliest frame of reference about the sexes.

What sort of body image did you develop? Many of the words we use to describe ourselves and others have a gender loading. For example, men built with a light frame and bone structure can be referred to as weedy, whereas women of a similar build are called petite. To be described as very tall is often thought to be a compliment to a man and a handicap to a woman. Heavily-built men are 'burly' and women 'butch'. To

_____

describe a baby boy as pretty feels very uncomfortable to his mother.

We all feel more secure the nearer we match to some generally accepted ideal, whatever we perceive that to be. Different eras and cultures see differently. Some see fat women as beautiful, but this is not so in current western images. How content are you with your facial features? Very many people feel that their ears, nose, mouth, or chin are too large or too small. Who set the standards for us, and how old were we when we began to judge ourselves in that way?

I still remember my acute embarrassment at being one of the earliest in my class to develop breasts. It made communal changing rooms for swimming or for trying on clothes a misery to me for years, and I developed a way of holding myself with rounded shoulders to try to hid my protruberances. On the other hand, a friend of mine had the opposite experience. She enjoyed her early developed breasts, and found them a status symbol in her class.

The other day I heard someone say that as a child his brother had told him that he had a big nose. After that, whenever he looked in the mirror he saw his nose first. When he looked at other people he compared his nose with theirs. If theirs was smaller he was slightly envious, and if larger he felt one up. It was only a momentary thought, but it was always with him. In fact, I had not noticed his nose as being in any way unusual.

One of the most freeing experiences about falling in love and being loved in return is that you love each other just the way you are. That brings with it a new confidence and radiance. These qualities shine in a newly-married couple as they walk down the aisle together and greet their friends at the wedding reception. They actually look more beautiful or handsome than usual, and it is not just the dress that does it!

These heightened feelings of being loved and lovable, just as we are, find expression in the sex act. The 'as we are' is naked and unashamed, and our closeness is in the embrace. Our giving and receiving is in the act itself, and we engage with our bodies and our hearts. I believe it to be a very different experience from 'having sex' as a physical meeting without commitment.

The sex act takes us into a physical loss of control, when involuntary muscles and reactions take over and in a sense possess us. When we are fully committed to the person who is helping us into that state, we can match the physical loss of control with an emotional abandonment in trusting love. The greater that sense of abandonment, the more we will find it to be a fulfilling experience, one in which we find ourselves by letting go of ourselves. In our union the boundary between us seems to melt for a few moments and we are not sure where we end and our partner begins. We feel fused and at one.

Strangely, the nearest we have been before to that kind of experience was during that 'moment of bliss' as a tiny baby, which I described in Chapter 2. At that time we would certainly not have described those feelings as sexual — if we had been able to describe them. But there is a deep similarity in the feeling of fulfilment at being known. Then too we were vulnerable, out of control, fully accepted and in union with another person, as a kind of extension of them. In fact, in the common sixteenth-century language of the Authorised Version of the Bible 'to know' someone meant to have sex with them.

For many couples sex happens just like this, at least some of the time. But the sexual act is a very delicate and variable experience. All that we feel about ourselves and our bodies, and all that our parents have modelled to us about sex and gender gets into bed with us. As my tutor used to say, 'Every time you make love there are at least eight people in the bed: you and your "inner child", your partner and their "inner child", and both sets of parents!' She was referring to what psychologists call the 'internalized' child or parent within each of us, which holds our past experience of those two roles. For people who have had sexual experiences with a number of partners the bed is even fuller, though this is not a thought we like to admit to. Even so, our denying it does not vanish it from our subconscious.

We learn to handle these 'presences' by pushing them down, along with the emotions attached to them. We split them off from our consciousness. Our bodies usually allow us to function on a physical level and have sex with an ensuing sense of physical satisfaction, without our having to become aware of the full range and content of our emotions. What is happening to our emotions at the time is unknown to us, and well-being in that area can be very uncertain. We may sometimes experience a sense of fragmentation along with the satisfaction, and a feeling of being in two minds. There may also be unbidden feelings of guilt or fear, which we will want to suppress.

Sex without commitment to a long-term relationship is in this divided state of mind, and in a sense it has to be. If the security of mutual commitment is not there, our 'unconscious' will not let us put ourselves, heart and soul, into the experience, even though we may believe ourselves to be totally involved.

Even sex within a permanent relationship can be affected by this same split. Most men find it easier than women to make this split within themselves, and many complex biological and psychological reasons are offered to explain this. At its most primitive, the need for the human race to reproduce itself is preserved by the male physicality, and the need for the young to be emotionally and physically parented for many years is protected by the slower response and greater emotional investment of the female in the sex act. But both men and women alike speak of a different kind of satisfaction when their bodies, minds, and spirits are caught up into their sexual experiences.

The sex act may follow on from a time of mutual sharing of ideas, or emotions, or spiritual perceptions. It may be a further expression of consolation at some sadness, or a way of completing the resolution of a quarrel. It may be an expression of the fun we find with our partner, or the love we want to show that way because they arouse us and attract us. But it may also be some sort of cry for help, like 'I am needing you to love me because I'm feeling unlovable.' Then the sex act can become a sort of yardstick to measure 'the amount you love me'. Or it may be that I am needing affirmation that I am 'a real man' or 'a real woman' and looking to sex to give me that. These different motives have their own dynamic which makes the kind of satisfaction we receive from the act different in each case. At an unconscious level we can be experiencing a movement towards a wholeness of personality — body, mind and spirit — or towards the reinforcing of bad feelings about ourselves.

Thinking back to all those people in bed with us when we make love, and our childhood and adolescent feelings about our own gender and the opposite sex, it should not surprise us to find that past unresolved hurts can break through our defences when we allow ourselves to be as vulnerable and exposed as the sex act requires. It may be that our suppressed emotions will not always allow us to make that artificial divide between the physical act of sex and its emotional implications, and so our 'performance' suffers.

Then men may find that they cannot get an erection, or that they get an ejaculation too soon, either outside the vagina or almost immediately upon entry. Women may find that it is very hard for them to relax the vaginal muscles enough to allow for penetration, or that they produce very little vaginal lubrication. One woman described her womb to me as a dried prune. That was saying much more about her emotional self-image than about her physical state. With these difficulties intercourse either does not happen, or happens with feelings of failure, hurt, and resentment.

When men 'fail' they are very exposed. An erection or lack of it is known about by both partners. Women can and do say that they have experienced an orgasm when they have not. Either party tends to compensate for their vulnerability by blaming the other for being too slow, or for not knowing how to arouse them, which may or may not be true.

When couples experience difficulties of this kind it strains the marriage. Books on sexual techniques may sometimes help, but more than anything else the pressure to succeed needs to be taken out of the situation. Unfortunately, some partners feel at this point that they have made a terrible mistake with the marriage, and that divorce is the only way out. But we take ourselves with us, and a divorce will rob the couple of the chance to work through old pains and hurts to a place of inner healing. Though one partner is often perceived by both as having the problem, there has usually been something in their unconscious choice of one another which means that there is a shared element in the difficulty.

Taking the pressure off the sex act can be experienced by widening the possibilities for mutual enjoyment, and at the same time building up physical trust and confidence in one another's bodies. Couples develop this by exploring each other's bodies through stroking and massage, and so learning to give and receive other sensations of physical pleasure and arousal. It can include manual excitement of the sex organs. Sex therapists sometimes advise this kind of exploration, and they often begin by excluding any attempt at intercourse, even by mutual masturbation, so as to free the experience from any kind of pressure to succeed until both partners are feeling more relaxed and safe.

But it is not just in cases of difficulty that we need to develop our enjoyment of touching and being touched. Quite often one partner, in a relationship where the shared sexual experience includes climaxing for both partners, complains that there is not enough foreplay for them, and that they find this a much more cherishing part of sex. We call a scene which arouses our emotions 'touching', but many of us are fairly out of touch with the connection between our bodies and our emotions.

Quite apart from learning to touch as a way of widening our enjoyment or cherishing our partner, it is also a psychological need. Some years ago experiments were carried out on a group of monkeys which demonstrated the connection between touch and sexual functioning.[1] A group of baby monkeys were reared without their mothers or mother figures. They were given substitute 'mothers' made out of wire. Some of these wire dummies were given a lactating nipple so that the babies could feed, and other dummies had no nipple but were covered with a terry towelling padding. The monkeys preferred the cloth monkeys and would only go to the nipple for food. If possible they would try to stay on a cloth monkey and lean over to reach the nipple on a wire monkey. In addition, the cloth monkeys gave the babies a greater sense of security in fear-arousing situations. As adolescents and adults none of these monkeys were able to perform sexually in a normal manner, even though they had not been kept away from the sight of other monkeys acting sexually together.

Many of us have grown up in 'very British' society having had to make do with very little touching in our childhood, but we can be enriched by experiencing more of it. I remember a vicar remarking that when he shook hands with his parishioners after church, he was aware that for some of the single and widowed people among them that handshake might be the only experience of touch they would have all week. No wonder that people from other cultures, where hugging is more natural, experience the British as cold.

Problems such as I have described are more likely to present themselves at the beginning of the sexual relationship. We may also be wanting help of a more medical kind over contraceptive methods, fertility, or infection. Because our sexuality is so much a part of our very identity and being, it will also touch upon our religious faith and our philosophy of life. In other words, different kinds of help may be needed, but there is a minefield of hidden thoughts and feelings here which can make something lovely into an experience of fear and rejection, and which will not improve by being ignored. Hard though it may be to discuss sexual difficulties — and it can feel threatening to the relationship to do it together — it is important to find the appropriate help. That help needs to include the finding of less threatening ways of sharing the problem with one's partner because, in the end, that is where the sharing needs to take place.

But many couples whose sex life is not good can often look back to an earlier period in their relationship when sex was satisfying for both of them. 'But now,' they say, 'something has changed between us. Maybe we are becoming bored with one another.' Desire has turned into tiredness, and tiredness into feelings of rejection. One partner may complain of feeling used by the other. Or a lack of spontaneity between them may be blamed on to a contraceptive device, which one of them resents having to use. Or an unexpressed ambivalence about having children may become focused in finding it a 'turn-off' to take temperatures and count the days since the last period. Either or both of them are tense and anxious, and feeling some resentment towards each other.

Often these are superficial difficulties, covering deeper feelings. The couple are having difficulties in other areas of their life together, which they may be expressing in a general bickering or in explosive rows, or by silent withdrawal and resentment. Then the unresolved anger, whether expressed or not, prevents a sharing of the tenderness which is essential for mutual sexual satisfaction. Sometimes one or both partners may feel that to have sex at this point would be to pretend to be close when they are emotionally far apart. It would feel like a loss of integrity and truth in their relationship. Or one may use their withholding from the sex act as a kind of punishment to the other for causing them hurt. Or the angry feelings may find expression by one of them forcing themselves on an unwilling partner, who then experiences emotions ranging from being used to being raped.

Here, as in other conflict situations, the temptation to project all the blame on to our partner is all too real, and feelings of being hurt and misunderstood can inflate at an alarming rate. 'I'm too tired', when repeated frequently, or 'you don't turn me on any more' become excuses for not facing the underlying emotional anxiety or conflict in the relationship.

I think of a young couple whose sex life was extremely fraught. They had three small children. The wife spoke of her husband's overbearing demands on her in bed, and more recently of an affair he had had with another woman. The wife, Liz, was a much more articulate person than her husband. She was very quick with words, while Frank was slow and unsure of himself. When they had arguments she could always win with words, and he was left feeling defeated and misunderstood. Physically, he was a big strong man and his physique was an important part of his well-being.

Frank's father was a long-distance lorry driver and when Frank was small, his father had often taken him on the long runs for company. The father and son had been involved in two motorway accidents while the son was at primary school, and in the second one the son had suffered severe concussion. This resulted in a partial loss of memory about the past, so that when Frank returned to primary school after a few weeks recuperation, he could not remember people's names or recent happenings. Class mates were incredulous. 'Surely you remember when we all went . . . (to some event) . . . and you said . . . and I said . . .' and he looked blank. Some of them teased him in the merciless way that children can, and Frank began to feel incredibly slow and stupid.

These were the very feelings that his wife was arousing by her quickness with words. He had admired this in Liz when they first got married and wanted it to be a part of 'them', but she was quite unaware of the history of his feelings and had given no opportunities for him to grow more confident in expressing himself. As Frank's frustration increased, so he

––––––

resorted to the only power he felt he had: his physical strength. He began to force himself on Liz in bed, and at other times he felt so frustrated that he felt like hitting her. In fact he was not always able to restrain himself from doing so, even though he despised the aggression in himself. The 'affair' was a desperate attempt to feel he was a man and to be valued by a woman who used touch much more than words. He was not in love with her but he was needing her.

Of course this is not the whole story. Our difficulties are rarely so one-sided. There were other questions which this couple's relationship posed, such as why did Liz choose a man whom she could control with words, and what conscious and unconscious factors were at work in her? But it is an illustration of the way in which our past history gets into bed with us.

This book is not an analysis of sexual difficulties, nor would I attempt to write one. However, if I had to identify the most common underlying difficulty that I have seen in sexual problems, I think I would choose the presence of a strong parental attitude, sometimes called an 'internalized controlling parent', in the couple's behaviour towards each other. By this I mean that people often complain that their partner is behaving like a child, or a parent. We all need to give expression to the child in us at times, and at other times to play parent to each other. But too much of this lessens our ability to relate as adult to adult. 'Children' are not allowed to have sex with their 'parents'. Sex belongs to the adult world, and when the child/ parent relationship is too evident in the marriage, sex often becomes distasteful or difficult.

Of course the truth is that sexual feelings *were* present in the child/parent relationship. For example, we may have said as a child or heard other children say 'When I grow up I'm going to marry you, Mummy/Daddy.' Inside us, though at a sub-conscious level, we knew that this involved a death-wish to-wards the other parent, a competitive jealousy which was too hot to har.dle. Such feelings are also a move towards violating society's taboo by which we protect the young child from abuse. Or there may have been some degree of parental sexual abuse in our childhood experiences. It is small wonder then that the echoing of child/parent attitudes and conflicts in a marriage can stir up some bad sexual feelings.

Suppressed feelings of power and powerlessness can find an outlet in aggressive sexual behaviour. It may be in a desire to control, or even to give vent to an unconscious hate towards the opposite sex. When feelings of this kind are being acted out, the need for therapeutic help is urgent. There is damage being done to both partners when loving and hating are as entangled as that.

I have tried to point out both good and bad experiences of sex. Normal sexual feelings can slide up and down that scale at different stages in a relationship. They do not only slide downwards, and that can give hope to those who are frightened by the fear that 'something is dying between us'. But, as in other areas of difficulty, we need to find a way of talking about it so that hurts and misunderstandings can be shared while we are still able to hold on to our respect for each other, and our belief in the other's better intentions.

The facts about our friends' relationships are so private to them that we can only use our vivid imaginations to fantasize about what other people may experience. But these fantasies affect our expectations for ourselves deeply. We are also affected by society's expectations, but I want to explore this more fully in the following chapter.

8

Children of our generation

The joys and hazards of sex are a part of the facts of life, but unfortunately our schools strengthen the false split between our bodies and emotions by teaching children about sex as a part of biology, and then referring to it as the 'facts of life'. The permissive nature of our society, which has grown together with 'safe' contraception, also reinforces the split, because sex can so easily be experienced without commitment. The media confirm the split by taking sex out of its natural setting. Sometimes we see it in a violent setting, such as a rape situation. Sometimes it is violent in a more covert way, with rough or even brutal handling, and with hard language, all designed to wind up the viewers' emotions. At other times sex is clothed in romance, with soft lights, beautiful hairdos, and designer nightwear. Both the violent and the romantic tap into sexual fantasies. We do not often see dramatic representations of the sexual relationship in an average and normal setting.

We are bombarded with sexually-loaded themes, coming at us from all sides. They come to us daily through radio and television, in magazines and advertising, and in song, from the moment we have eyes to see and ears to hear.

Violence brings with it a dimension of fear, along with some 'macho' fantasies. It denies tenderness and vulnerability. Romance offers a picture of instant success, and therefore carries a great investment in first impressions, and how you look. With that, inevitably, comes the fear of instant failure and rejection. Both violence and romance remove sex from the process of 'learning to know you as a unique person and loving you the way you are'. Both do violence to true respect and intimacy, and when fantasy becomes our reality we are in trouble.

When John McCarthy was interviewed on television by Michael Aspel[1] about his experiences during the five years he spent as a hostage, John was asked what changes he had noticed in everyday life when he was released. His immediate response was to comment on the increase in sexually explicit scenes on television. I myself had not thought that the last five years had shown much change, but his remark highlighted for me the fact that we are not able to measure change when it is happening all around us. Even so we are still affected by it.

We are children of our generation and we cannot avoid being influenced by its philosophy. Sigmund Freud spoke of 'collective neurosis', and perhaps this splitting of the body-mind-spirit nature of the sexual experience is a part of that. The full sexual experience, born out of love and commitment, is enriched when the relationship has weathered storms and conflict and stood the test of time. It does not lead to boredom with one another. History and literature bear witness to this. As an example I quote from a letter by Karl Marx to his wife. They had been married thirteen years and she was away visiting her dying mother:

> There are actually many females in the world, and some of them are beautiful. But where could I find again a face whose every feature, even every wrinkle, is a reminder of the greatest and sweetest memories of my life? Even my endless pains, my irreplaceable losses, I read in your sweet countenance, and I kiss away the pain when I kiss your sweet face . . .[2]

This is obviously written in a moment of passion, when he was missing her presence, but there is something important here about joy and pain being an inseparable part of each other.

But I have seen couples who after a very few years of marriage have lost hope in their relationship. They cannot see the possibility of it bringing them joy any more, and they feel that divorce is their only solution. They had high hopes when they set out together, and both feel that they have worked at their relationship. But the changes that each has been trying to make, partly in themselves and more often in their partner, have not taken place. Maybe there has been a little improvement, at times, but it is not enough and they have lost hope in the process of marriage adjustment and growing together. They say that their marriage is not a success and it has not worked out.

Sometimes I feel that there are deep-seated difficulties which are damaging to the relationship, but at other times I have felt that they are the victims of society's current philosophy. I believe that we are all more conditioned than we realize, and society today thinks in a very short-term way. We therefore find it more difficult to take on board the idea of short-term loss for long-term gain. Yet this is a necessary ingredient in the growth of relationships and especially of marriage.

Life today does not offer much long-term hope, and this is reflected at every level. The political party in power has a five-year term, and policies brought in towards the end of that term are influenced by their members' desire to be re-elected. The long-term good of the country has to be set aside. Nationally and internationally we are used to 'crisis government', which is a response to immediate situations. The crisis so absorbs our thinking that we are not able to have much concern for the future.

Speed has become very important to us. We have 'instant' everything. Obsolescence is built into our manufacturing and the 'life' of a machine gets shorter and shorter. Our childhoods are littered with throwaway toys.

Society today tends to view difficulties as mistakes which ought to have been avoided, rather than opportunities for

---

learning. In politics and in the business world a mistake is often placed on a scapegoat and that person is asked to resign. Then life goes on as usual, even though a whole department may be at fault.

The insurance world plays on the idea that difficulties ought not to exist, by encouraging us to insure against every hardship. An easy life is not only the best, but a right: 'You owe it to yourself . . ' I am not saying this against the principle of insurance, which is a necessity of modern life, but I am wanting to highlight the subtle influences that play upon us through advertising and have an effect on the way we think.

With all this, is it surprising if we are losing touch with the basic principles of growth for all living things, both plants and people? We have become separated from the time-scale and the hope which is built into creation; that from apparent leaflessness and deadness comes increased vigour and resilience to life. Growth has its own necessary cycle, and hard times are not a big mistake. In the area of physical well-being we cannot deny the importance of difficulty. We know that physical exercises which take us to the limit of our strength increase our capacity. But somehow we do not apply that to the growth of relationships, whether at home or at work.

Yet the great world religions all affirm this principle of life. Christianity holds it as a central belief through the life of Christ. His new and greater influence for good, the life of his Spirit, was released after the resurrection and came as a result of his obedience to his way of life. Being of one mind and heart with his father he therefore chose the way of obedience to the divine process of life through death. The seed must die to bring forth fruit.[3] Every short-term sacrifice is a little death for a greater life and a greater love; this is the long-term gain. Every parent does this when they see that their children have enough food even if they themselves go short.

But somewhere along the line religion has turned this life-affirming process into a self-destructive masochistic one. Sometimes it has glorified hardship as though it were an end in itself, and not a route to life. Our present-day secular society has sought to set us free from this gloomy bondage, and yet it has produced a new bondage of its own, and one which is very short on hope for the future or belief in the process of creative change.

But although some marriages are falling apart for lack of hope, we also see marriages that are self-evidently strengthened through difficulty. There is something to learn here about attitudes and their power over us. 'As we think, so we become.' Difficulties which stem from childhood, such as have been described in earlier chapters, are certainly the greatest influence on us, but each of us needs to become more aware of the outside influences upon us and the ways in which we are all children of our generation.

In Victorian times society shrouded sex with secrecy. This meant that men, women, and children — and perhaps women in particular — could be used and abused in all manner of ways. It has gradually become clear that there was a great deal of untold suffering. The openness with which society now treats sex means that the abuse of it need no longer go untold. There are safe havens, support groups and helplines available which never existed before. Abuse can be owned or exposed and further suffering lessened. This is certainly an improvement on the past and, in this respect, we are a much more humane society.

On the other hand, that very openness has made possible the constant display of sexually-evocative pictures, films, magazines, advertisement hoardings and music which can produce an arousal of sexual feelings with nowhere to go.

The Song of Songs, which is an erotic love song in the Old Testament, has a relevant comment on this. The Song expresses passionate feelings between the lover and his beloved:

My lover is to me a sachet of myrrh resting between my breasts.

How beautiful you are, my darling! . . . Your eyes are like doves.

How handsome you are, my lover! Oh, how charming! . . . our bed is verdant.

The poetic imagery continues in this way throughout the Song, but twice a warning is included:

Daughters of Jerusalem, I charge you . . . do not . . . awaken love until it so desires.[4]

What can anyone do with wound-up sexual feelings which have not been drawn out by a real person? Where can they go, other than into superficial and distorted sexual relationships, or into the flights of fantasy?

Sexual fantasies are one-sided and untested, and so they can create unreal expectations in us. These can affect us when we enter a loving relationship with a real person. We may find that our joint 'performance' is not up to our fantasy of the experience. We can then either lose confidence in our capacity to give pleasure or see our partner as not performing well enough for our fantasy. We can be haunted by pictures of what we imagine to be 'the real thing'. Past sexual relationships can also come into bed with us, as I mentioned before, as comparisons with what is happening in bed during the here and now. These thoughts can upset our ability to respond to a unique individual in a uniquely individual way.

There are programmed pictures in us of 'success' and 'failure' which we may be fighting hard to deal with even while we are having intercourse. People who have been married more than once will often have to struggle with these feelings in the early days of a new marriage.

If the sexual experiences being compared were from a time before marriage then there is another danger in the comparison. The fact of being committed carries with it a much greater vested interest in 'getting it right' in bed. This can make some people more tense and less physically free for a while. If they then make comparisons between physical success outside marriage when there was much less emotional invest-ment in the relationship, and in marriage when it matters to them very much, they may come to all the wrong conclusions. They may wonder if they are really suited to their marriage partner instead of recognizing that the possibilities for a really satisfying sex life together are far greater than in any tempor-ary involvement. However titillating that might have been, they now have the conditions for growth towards a full sexual experience which can take in the whole personality — body, mind, and spirit.

It would be a nonsense to say that all fantasy is bad, and so we need to identify what is happening inside us. Dreaming dreams is a very creative part of ourselves. We learn a great deal about life through identifying with other people. In fan-tasizing about ourselves, as heroes and lovers for example, we explore our feelings. The Song of Songs is in the Bible as a love song to be read.

I remember talking with a Christian friend many years ago about a public demand to ban *Lady Chatterley's Lover* by D. H. Lawrence. She told me that she had read it at a time when she was learning to cope with some very muddled sexual feelings and areas of ignorance within her during the early years of her marriage, and she had found it a great help. She remarked that it was only a dirty book if you were reading it to feed your own sexual fantasies in an unhelpful way.

Sometimes a sexually explicit book or film can show us new ways of being. It can help us to get in touch with a tenderness we have never experienced. In order to understand ourselves, we need to become more aware of the outside influences upon us as well as those from within. Then we can be awake to the kind of fantasy we are experiencing, and its connection with reality. We can also begin to distinguish the times when erotic fantasy is not helping us towards a real relationship, or to the integration within ourselves of our body, mind, and spirit.

When a married partner is having fantasies of sex with other people, it is often an expression of anger. It can be a sort of hidden punishment to their partner for upsetting them or a venting of frustration. As it is taking something away from the relationship, it is not enough to try to suppress the fantasy. Our guilty feelings will often drive us to do so, but it is more important to look for the real cause and try to deal with that.

Children growing up in our open and permissive society can be made aware of their physical potency long before their emotions have developed to a similar capacity. This in itself can be frightening, and can drive some teenagers into the 'safety' of same-sex physical relationships. It can be a way of running for cover in a world which overexposes them to their own sexuality. At least someone of the same sex seems more understandable than that other kind — the opposite sex — and some people can feel that through identifying with someone of their own sex they will learn more about their own sexual drives and emotions.

A homosexual stage, sometimes expressed in crushes on people, is a normal part of our sexual development. We need to find some degree of confidence in our own gender before we can make good relationships with the opposite sex. This confidence starts to grow in us through our relationship with our own parents, and to the extent that they are at ease with their own gender. This ease enables them to relate to us in a way which is neither cold, nor with incestuous overtones. We also draw from many other role models, real and imaginary. Learning about ourselves and our sexuality is a slow process, and as in every other area of learning, we develop at different rates.

In saying the above I am not making a general statement about homosexuality. I recognize a difference between those with a developmental problem such as I have described, and

those homosexuals and lesbians who recognize within themselves a settled sexual orientation, and who have confident
and easy friendships with members of both sexes. It is the
developmental problem which I see as increased by the heavy
sexual overloading which comes to us through the media.

The media also have an affect on our capacity to feel compassion. Day after day, and year after year, we see desperately
upsetting incidents on the news. We are witnesses to cruelty
and murder from our own armchairs. We can respond occasionally through one of the hundreds of charitable agencies,
but what is happening to our compassion? It is wound up, yet
with very little focus for its expression. I believe that this
produces a climate of general anxiety in us, and at the same
time deadens our person-to-person response.

I remember being shown a letter written by a mother to her
son during the seventies. She told how she had thought that
the advent of television would bring a change in people's
understanding of one another. We would learn about each
other's lives and become more tolerant. But now she realized
that this was not happening. In the old days neighbours in her
street had shown their compassion when someone died by
collecting for a street wreath and by providing meals for the
bereaved family. People were not bothering with that any
more.

There are, of course, other sociological changes which have
loosened the bonds of community among us, and maybe her
interpretation was oversimplified, but I can feel within myself
that growth of 'not bothering' in the face of so much need and
pain. Surely, this in some way affects my general capacity to
respond lovingly and sensitively to those nearest to me.

Compassion is at the heart of our loving someone, warts and
all. It goes together with our gratitude for their ability to make
similar allowances for us. It also presupposes our belief in their
worth as a person and our respect for that. It exercises our
ability to put ourselves in another person's shoes. When we see

a starving mother holding her dying child, we think, 'If that were me I couldn't bear the pain', and our own heart feels that pain in a minutely similar way. That is com-passion, the sharing of pain together *with* another.

Compassion is an essential ingredient in all relationships, let alone in marriage. It is about being human together. I believe that if some situation prompts us into action, whether that be to give money, write a letter, take flowers, be extra kind, make a cup of tea, or whatever, we should be faithful to ourselves and carry out that prompting. Otherwise we are encouraging a deadening of our responses and a 'don't care' outlook. If we do respond, we are developing within ourselves eyes that see and hearts that feel, and we will inevitably be more loving and more lovable ourselves.

9

Roles and reactions

Many years ago I knew a couple brought up in the 1920s. He was a London City Missioner and he saw his role in the home as the one who carried the coals, cleaned and lit the fire, and emptied the rubbish. They would usually have several people in to meals on a Sunday, and after tea he would sit by the fire while his wife waded through a mountain of washing-up. He never offered to help her. He felt quite comfortable about that not being his job, and his wife was comfortable with her role and very awkward when a male visitor offered to give her a hand. They both enjoyed a good and satisfying relationship, and were interesting people to visit.

Our idea about the 'appropriate role' for a man or a woman has changed very fast during this century. In the 1940s you rarely saw a man pushing a pram. As recently as the 1960s it was unusual for a woman to get a mortgage in her own right. Women are now in the areas of business and government as heads of departments, with authority over men, but there are still many men in mid-career who are finding themselves working for a woman boss for the first time. Sometimes this experience sets up very uncomfortable echoes from childhood, where they last felt under a woman's power. Even though a man may accept the idea of a woman in authority in principle, he may still experience a real difficulty with it in practice. He is then more likely to blame that particular woman for causing the problem than admit to a discomfort within himself. This highlights a tension within us between two different rates of change. We can adapt to the ideas and values which we have learnt about as adults much more easily than we can go against those we imbibed during our childhood.

As adults we will have developed many new ideas and beliefs. We will have learnt a great deal during our student days, and in vocational training. We will have taken part in discussions and formed our own opinions. We will have caught something of the general drift of society's thinking. Parliament is always having to legislate for changed attitudes; for example we now have an Equal Opportunities Act, and a race relations policy. But we only have to look at the television news, or at the emotions expressed over Northern Ireland, or into our own hearts, to see that we cannot make laws to ensure a change in personal feelings and emotions.

Somewhere inside us is another voice which seems to say 'as it was in the beginning, is now, and ever shall be'. It sounds as though it carries a God-like authority, and it sabotages our new thinking. It pushes us to 'revert to type', as it was in *our* beginning, at the foundation place of our security, and at the place where we first learned what it meant to be a man or a woman. And so when we look at our role as men or women in a changing society, we sometimes find ourselves in a state of tension and inner confusion. I see this tension expressing itself when couples are trying to work out their roles in marriage. It can cause hurt and misunderstanding between them, and arouse thoughts like 'If you really loved me you would know what kind of a role you should play towards me as a proper man/woman.'

I remember a young Indian couple, both educated for most of their childhood in England, whose families had known each other for years. Both married wanting to have a 'liberated western-style marriage, like the English couples we met at college', to use their own words. But in the event, the pressures from within them to conform to preconditioned roles made both of them very anxious, and produced endless arguments. One of their problems was that in their own culture parental

---

authority was strong, and was expected to continue after marriage. This was especially difficult for the husband, whose mother and father lived nearby, and it was undermining the contract that each had made to the other in getting married.

Cross-cultural marriages do carry an inherent tension, though the more obvious the cultural differences are, the more likely it is that the issues will have been discussed openly, and before the marriage. The less obvious truth is that every marriage is a cross-cultural event. The culture of our own family, its roles, its manners, its do's and don'ts, and its ways of communication can be poles apart from our partner's, even when couples come from the same class, race, and street. And it has to be said that changes in society sometimes take longer to filter down through some family systems than through the legal system!

For example, women are now educated for the same careers as men, and both have opportunities for promotion. When a couple get married they usually carry on with their jobs until the first child is nearly due and then the wife takes a break. At that stage one of them, and it can be either, may find that their feelings about both of them working and their baby being given into the care of a child-minder may be different, in the event, from their own past theoretical ideas about it. They may have spoken strongly in favour of it in the past, but when it happens in their own home one partner may find themselves in the grip of very uneasy feelings which they find difficult to voice.

We find it hard to admit the tensions in us between our logic and our emotions, especially as society seems to value 'head' talk more highly than 'heart' talk. We may keep repeating to ourselves all the reasonable arguments, and yet underneath that 'law' from our emotional roots suggests that there is another set of rules which we are breaking. In fact we feel very much 'in two minds'. This is another situation in which it is all too easy to throw the blame for the confusion on to our partner

---

instead of admitting our own state of mind. Because our roles are a part of our image of ourselves we are tempted to let ourselves be overinfluenced by our friends' opinions. We want their approval, and it takes some courage to handle the criticism of family and friends and stand our own ground.

Women staying at home with their children may be teased about being 'little women' or 'earth mothers', and women trying to hold on to a career may feel pressured into being superwoman, models of the modern liberated woman, yet striving to keep alive traditional ideas about a mother's role. Husbands can be unaware of the strain this can produce.

Sometimes the arrival of a baby does not present us with a choice. A shortage of money or a need to pay the mortgage is the deciding factor; that may be a reality for us which was not so for our parents. But even when that is the case it is still very important to share our feelings and our hopes. Otherwise we may have our private expectations for the future, and find that our partner always seems to be thwarting our plans. For example, a husband may be living with the secret hope that one day things may be different. Maybe he will have a financial windfall or earn more money. Then his wife could stop earning and he would be able to have a 'real wife' at home, and the children could have 'a real mother'. Then he would not have to spend so much of his time on household chores, and life would be much better for everyone. Unbeknown to him, his wife may be very pleased with the arrangements she has set up for the children. She may be enjoying her paid work and expecting promotion in the future. She may feel that the stimulus she gets from her work makes her a better wife and mother.

Or the scenario might be the other way round. The wife may be aiming to give up work as soon as their finances allow it. She may be wanting her husband to take on a better paid job or trying hard to simplify their lifestyle in order to save where possible. She is longing to be at home and to spend more time with the children. But her husband may not be

---

wanting to go into a job which carries more responsibility, or he may feel quite strongly that wives should earn a share of the family expenses. 'After all,' he may think, 'other men's wives do it, why not mine?' The husband may believe that being at home is a soft option; many men envy wives who are 'at home all day enjoying themselves'. It is not difficult to see where unexpressed hopes of this kind can lead. The whole superstructure of aims for the future can be built on false assumptions which have never been checked out.

There is fear and fantasy, envy and competition in the air over the question of roles in a marriage. These can also come to light when we are faced with a choice over which partner's career takes first place. Is it yours or mine? Who can take time off when the children are ill? Which career brings in the most money, or gives the family the most security or well-being? It may affect where we live. Does the vicar, whose wife has just been offered a headship at a school fifty miles away, look for another parish? And what things should they take into account when they make their choice?

In marriage we find that the unspoken contract which we entered into and the roles which we assumed for ourselves and each other soon need to be spoken about. The way we share out the tasks and take responsibilities may need to be clarified and amended in any stage in our life together (see the 'Pinch/ Crunch' chart in Chapter 4). Any change in our circumstances — a change of job, the birth of a child, the inclusion of an aged parent into the household, the onset of an illness, or even a windfall legacy — will affect both partners and needs to be discussed.

When a husband or wife considers how a change for them will affect their partner, by putting themselves into the other person's shoes and sharing their thoughts, that other person feels loved, and is much more likely to shoulder any new difficulties with a good spirit than when they feel taken for granted and their good will assumed. In fact any role which one partner performs for the benefit of the couple is in some way a gift to the other, and needs to be acknowledged from time to time. If we do not do this, we are in danger of not respecting one another and of not living out *our* marriage. In fact we may well be comforming to other people's notions about marriage, or responding to ideals born of our parents' marriages which worked for them in their generation.

Many people are wondering today if full employment will ever be possible again, when so many jobs can be done more cheaply and quickly by machines. There are families in the north-east of England and in other areas where three generations of men have not had paid jobs. They have no work role or status. Redundancy and unemployment place an enormous strain on married life, putting at risk the satisfaction of the only roles left to those men, as a husband, father, and a member of their community. It calls for courage and creative thinking to address this problem, but politicians keep implying that full employment will one day return. The difficulty with living as though a job might be round the corner is that we cannot then grieve the loss of our work role, let go of it, and create new patterns and roles for living. But is it appropriate to give up hope? Will society reject such people as lazy ne'er-do-wells, or has it already done so?

Counsellors have observed an increase in sexual dysfunction among men who have been made redundant. Their impotence to influence their work situation can bring on an impotence in their ability to function sexually. Our roles and our image of ourselves as men and women are deeply entwined at every level of our being.

Working out the roles in a marriage raises the questions of who takes the power and control over what. How are decisions reached about how much time is spent with in-laws, or about social commitments, or the style of entertaining? Who decides how the money is to be spent, and makes the choices? How free does either partner feel to spend money without consultation?

Often in a counselling situation a partner will express resentment at the way the other one controls their life when they have never mentioned it to their partner before. The exchange goes like this: 'You never said, you let me think you liked it that way', and the other replies, 'I knew you wanted it that way, so I just went along with it.'

This 'anything for a quiet life' attitude is not a real kindness to themselves or their partners. A husband said one day, 'You always make such a fuss about entertaining, everything has got to be just right. I like a much more informal way of having friends in, but you have to go over the top and it costs us a fortune.' And she replied, 'That's the first time you ever said that, you always seem to enjoy it a lot.'

On another occasion the wife said, 'I really resent the way you take your mother shopping every Saturday morning. It cuts into our weekend together, and I think she's being very selfish', and her husband replied, 'I thought you liked that time to yourself to sort out the house before the weekend. You never said this before.'

What chance has either partner given each other if they do not communicate? A marriage breakup sometimes appears to 'come out of the blue', but I wonder if that is very likely. Perhaps it could be so in the case of a sudden infatuation, but it is much more likely to come as a result of non-communication; out of irritations and unmet needs that have never been shared, and have therefore never been given a chance to be met.

The role that either partner takes up over money varies a great deal between marriages. Some couples talk about 'your money and my money', others say 'our money'. Sometimes one partner always supplies the pressure to save and the other the pressure to spend. It may be that there is an unspoken mistrust in one of the other's tendency to overspend or to be mean. We are different from one another in the areas where we can allow ourselves to be self-indulgent, and in the areas where we spend sparingly and think that other people are extravagant. Couples are fortunate when these happen to coincide. But interdependence over money can be very risky, especially when money is short. The controller of the purse is in a powerful position and so is the earner of the money.

John and Betty's marriage showed a daily tension over money and decision-making. John had been brought up in very poor circumstances and was understandably afraid of a shortage of money. He was out of work when I met them, but had inherited a small private income through a distant relative. Betty had worked more or less full-time, but recently her job had come to an end and she only had a little part-time work. Betty was a strong person, who took the major role in organizing their family life, but there were times when John stolidly refused to be organized. However, John controlled the money, and Betty felt like a little girl being given her pocket money each week. He did most of the food shopping, arguing that he had the time and skill to do it; he was adamant about not having a joint account.

Their marriage was fraught with constant arguments, each having their own position of power from the role they assumed. But though they had some violent battles, there were ways in which it suited them both to keep it that way. John was socially shy, and in many ways it suited him for Betty to be the organiser and social contact maker. Betty's widowed mother had some unreal expectations about Betty's duty to help her financially, and it suited Betty to be able to say truthfully that she had no control over their money. In this way their marriage had an uneasy balance of power through the roles they each took up. This made it very difficult indeed for either of them to change, even though both were dissatisfied with the relationship. The inflexibility of their roles was only a symptom of their previous deprivation as children. The healing which their relationship needed was at a much deeper level than could have been reached by trying to alter their roles.

———

When we guard our roles jealously, it is often an expression of our fear. We may feel the need to be in control or we may feel that we are only of value because of what we do, and if our partner develops our particular skill or takes on our role, they will be less dependent on us. Some of us need to be needed and we have to keep it that way. But the varying of roles within marriage can be a very creative experience. It can help us to experiment and learn new skills. It can increase our appreciation of one another and our trust. It can give family life more flexibility. In the safety of our home we can make mistakes and grow in confidence with each other's help. This is assuming that we can tolerate one another's mistakes, and not behave like the critical parent or elder brother who may have undermined our confidence in childhood.

There is real opportunity here for the healing of past childhood hurts and the reworking of our self-esteem, if we can work it out within each other's trust and love. But I would not want to deny that many conflicts over roles are but the 'tip of the iceberg', and may lead us to look at deeper insecurities.

———

10

Conflict: 'It's much worse than I thought'

I hope the reader can resist the temptation to read this chapter first. I have left it until now as it will make more sense in the light of previous chapters.

Anger is a powerful weapon for change, which can be both creative and destructive. Each of us sees our own anger in a very different light from that of our partner. My anger is a very strong and serious emotion, which can feel quite violent at times, but *my* anger feels justified and therefore reasonable. It feels as though I am defending myself and fighting for my life, and if I do not win I will go under. I am not attacking you, only defending myself. *Your* anger feels quite unreasonable, very attacking, and often rather trivial. This is a common frame of mind when we are having a row, and I think it will have a familiar ring for most of us.

As I have said a number of times, the energy of a current emotion is not just created out of the present situation but is fuelled by past unexpressed feelings, often stemming from early childhood. This is true of anger. It is as if an inner voice is saying,

When I was a child 'they' attacked me, and I wasn't big enough to defend myself. I was at their mercy, and had to comply to their will. But I'm grown up now, and I'm not going to be pushed around any more. I'm going to take my place in the world and have my rightful power. I will not sit down under anyone.

The 'you' with whom I am having a row becomes a part of 'them': those people who have always thwarted me, and not understood or valued me. So the battle starts from a place where listening is inevitably difficult, since 'you' are not a reasonable individual but a part of that gang against me, whereas 'I' am very much an individual, and all alone. And of course that frame of mind goes for both of us. The agenda for the row could be anything, but the moment the row starts, it evokes our hurt feelings. We begin to feel unloved and that brings up a second agenda. It becomes quite different from other rows, at work for example, because we feel that this person, my partner of all people, should not want to hurt me but to love me.

In fact the love we are hoping for in marriage is often measured against a scale of childhood needs. It can be that our backlog of being misunderstood seems so large, and our experience of unconditional love so small, that it feels outrageous that here in marriage, where we are counting on love and understanding, we should meet the same old lack of support.

Inside many people is a dark well-hole of need for love. Even good parenting cannot be all sufficient, but some have gone through childhood very short on unconditional love and their well feels bottomless. This well-hole, whatever its depth, feels like an open mouth hungry for nourishment. When we meet someone whom we believe has just the kind of love we need, our expectations go up enormously. Sometimes our partner gives us what feels like a reasonable meal of love and we are temporarily satisfied, but at other times they just give us 'a little bit of love', which may be all they can spare for the moment. That titbit only reminds us of the sweet taste of love without satisfying our hunger, and it can feel like an insult in the face of our need. Then our anger rises, and we feel or say 'Do you call that love!' and throw it back in their face.

At that moment we are hating the other person as the one who could meet our need, but refuses to do so. Love and hate can be two sides of the same penny. It is only because the love has been there and now seems to be withheld that we hate them for it.

Most of us have great difficulty in using such a strong word as 'hate' to describe our feelings. It is a 'bad' word, and it makes us feel guilty. We are not supposed to hate in families. In any case we are busy seeing our partner's nastiness, and if we recognize our own hate or guilt we shall lose the battle. So we deny it to ourselves. But of course we have already communicated it in thinking or saying 'Do you call that love!', and our partner will pick it up somehow. Even a jerk of the head can give the message. It is a moment of 'intense dislike', which is the dictionary meaning of hate — and our partner will react accordingly.

Paradoxically, since I have learnt to recognize hate within myself I have become more at peace. I am not pleased to find it inside me, but denying it was not allowing me to have 'truth in the inward parts'. I feel that owning it has been a growth towards wholeness and integrity. It has made me more tolerant of those I love, and more able to recognize their moments of hate for what they are. And so often they are fleeting moments of intense feeling born out of past experiences of powerlessness and anger and hurt.

In theory we know that every marriage has its differences, but when we are facing our own, they feel much more painful than we had expected. This is made worse by the fact that we see our partner as the one who started the battle. However, once conflict is set up we are likely to deal with it in whatever way we learned from our past experience.

One couple I know were married for five years before they could express their feelings in an argument. Greg had grown up as the mediator between his two parents. Argument was terrible in his experience. Rows could develop into two weeks of silent anger in which all messages between the parents were delivered through him. He would sit at supper being spoken to by both parents, who were still refusing to speak to each other. Because of the pain of that experience he vowed to himself that when he got married he would never have a row.

His wife, Pat, came from a volatile family where everyone spoke at once and no one listened very much. She was used to bickering and sparring within the family as a way of making oneself heard. Rows were 'no big deal', but a very necessary part of life. Pat tried and tried to get a reaction from Greg. She wanted to express their areas of conflict and work through them to a place of mutual understanding. Greg felt that the marriage would be at an end once they had a row, and when any conflict was in the air he would go silent or walk away from it.

Pat goaded and goaded Greg, until one morning he burst. He shouted at Pat, looked as though he would explode with anger, and then he left the house for work, slamming the front door. He felt dreadful all day and overwhelmed with fear for their future. Pat felt something relax inside her for the first time. She had been heard. She had got through at last. Now perhaps they could have a decent argument and resolve their differences. When Greg came home he was amazed at Pat's relaxed and almost happy state. He had expected silence and hatred. Then he told Pat about his fears of coming home and she in turn was very surprised.

This was the beginning of a new way of being together for both of them. Greg learned that conflict was not the end of the marriage, and Pat learned a greater respect for his feelings. It did not mean that arguments were no longer threatening, but it did mean that they could be tolerated and handled better by them both.

In the same way that we develop methods of defending ourselves as children, so we develop ploys for getting our own way. When we fight one another in marriage we get out our old weapons. Survival is the name of the game and we are determined to get our own way rather than go under. There are a number of recognizable weapons used in our battles and I will mention some of them below.

Bullying   We may have learnt that the only way we could get what we wanted was by force. Maybe we saw this modelled at home, or we might have developed it in response to a weak or fearful parent. But whatever the reason we have found that bullying works for us. It stops us from recognizing our own very frightened 'child' inside. We would not admit that we have become a bully, but just occasionally we may get a glimpse of ourselves as others see us and know that this is true. 'Blowing your top' is a form of bullying. The message is 'If you engage in battle with me now, you will get hurt!'

Sulking   Here we withhold our love and our good spirits in order to bring our partner to heel. If our partner has experienced 'withholding love' at home, this can be a very powerful weapon.

Wheedling or Nagging   We won't let the matter rest until we get our own way. No doubt we have seen children doing this to their parents in toy shops, and we may have learnt that way as a child. It plays on the parent's or partner's guilt, and although we may win, they are often left feeling angry.

Stone-walling   We can get our own way by being immovable, and blocking the other person. We will not discuss the matter. Our minds are made up. We do not want to know what they think.

Guilt-making   This is a very powerful weapon with a moral 'edge' to it. We sometimes use it consciously, but more often unconsciously. We say 'You ought . . . you haven't . . . and you should . . .' There is a great deal of latent guilt in us all, and if we can tap the guilt in our partner we can often put pressure on them. It is as if we are putting ourselves on God's side, so that he can do the fighting for us, and the chances are that we will get our own way! It evokes a child/parent response between us. Most of us were told as children that we ought and we shouldn't, and if we become the 'parental voice' our partner may obey us but feel belittled. Of course there may be moral issues in our discussion, but we can only address them freely from a place of equality before God and between ourselves. A 'holier than thou' attitude is harmful to both partners.

Sarcasm   This is a real put-down, aiming to make the partner feel stupid. For those who had an academic struggle at school, or who for any reason felt stupid as children, this can be like pulling the rug from under their feet.

Placating   This is used by people who are very frightened of confrontation or conflict. It is not the same as peacemaking, where differences are acknowledged and valued. Placaters will minimize or deny differences of opinion. They will apologize when they do not feel to blame, because they are wanting to kiss and make up. They will do almost anything to avoid conflict. If they keep succeeding in their ploy there will be a build-up of suppressed anger in the relationship, which may be shattering if it finally erupts, or drive the partners apart if it does not.

Purely logical reasoning   This is used by someone who solves problems without allowing feelings or emotion to have any weight. For them, what has no known reason is unreliable and dangerous. This is the sort of argument which says 'You should not be frightened because there is nothing to be frightened of'. The development of this attitude can sometimes be traced back to a very emotional parent; perhaps one who often burst into tears, or who used emotional blackmail to get their own way. The child is at the mercy of something so beyond its understanding, so irrational, that it determines never to get into the grip of another person's emotions again. Unfortunately, what is conveyed to the partner is a coldness which denies emotion and therefore seems to deny love.

Knowing our partner well means that we will know their vulnerability and just how to wind them up. They may lose their temper or lose their ground, leaving us feeling that we have the moral high ground. They have lost control, whereas we have not. They are being childish but we are behaving like adults, so we tell ourselves.

In the privacy of reading this book, it may be a help to you to pause here, and try to identify which of these weapons you know how to use, and how you would feel without them. A change in a method of fighting will be very risky, but on the whole none of these weapons makes for a creative conflict.

But there are ways of handling conflict which can strengthen a couple's relationship and help them to develop their trust and love. There are some 'Queensberry Rules' which can turn our dirty fighting into a clean and fair fight. Both partners may still feel bruised in the process, but there need be no lack of respect at the end of it.

At the beginning of this chapter I highlighted the different fantasies we have about our own anger and our partner's anger: *I* am alone, reasonable, serious, and defending myself, but *you* are being unreasonable, bigoted, trivial, attacking, and one of the old gang.

If anything creative is going to happen in our row, there has to be a change in those perceptions. Each has to look at the other person again, and see them as they are, an individual who is alone. The word 'respect' comes from a root meaning 'to look again', and unless we both have an adequate respect for the other person as an individual, we can destroy each other. We also have to recognize that they, like us, believe that they are not attacking us but are defending themselves, and that they feel very justified and serious about it. This way we are giving our partner the same ground to stand on as we give ourselves.

Another requirement for creative change is that we try to stretch our ability to listen. Only by listening hard can we hear something new which might change the situation, but of

———

course the more we feel we need to defend ourselves, the harder it is to listen. For this reason it may be useless to continue trying to resolve anything when feelings run too high. We may need to cool off and come back into the ring for another try in ten minutes or two hours time. We shall not only need to listen, but to ask questions to test that we have heard correctly. Sometimes we can repeat what they have said back to them in other words: 'Are you saying that you . . .?' 'Do you feel . . .?' We can afford to do plenty of this because it often reveals that we are talking at cross purposes.

We will need to tell the other person about our own feelings. This is sometimes referred to as giving 'I' messages, instead of 'you' messages, and it can completely alter the way an argument goes. As an example, let us suppose that a husband comes in late from work not having phoned his wife to let her know, and that the supper is now spoilt. 'You' messages might go like this:

> You're late, you never rang and you got me really worried. How do you expect me to give you a nice meal at this hour! I've been keeping it warm for the last two hours.

The response to that, whether spoken or unspoken, could well be:

> Why does she always have to bitch at me and make herself into a martyr? If she had any love for me she would know that I'm tired and very hungry.

The wife might get a sullen apology from him, but not much else. An 'I' message might be:

> I had no idea you were going to be so late. The dinner has been in the oven since eight o'clock and I'm afraid it's ruined. In the last hour I began to get really worried.

———

This message is free from blame. It communicates most of the wife's feelings, but in holding back the anger it gives the husband the space to respond quite differently. He may then feel genuinely sorry about her anxiety and her wasted efforts and want to say so. She knows a real sorry from a placating one and feels respected. She may then say, 'You look whacked. What kept you?' And he will be able to reply without being defensive.

'I' messages make us communicate our own feelings and take responsibility for them. They give others information about us. That means we are being more open. They suspend blame and improve trust. They help good communication. 'You' messages do the opposite. They 'get at' other people and make critical judgements. They give very little information about ourselves and block further discussion. A change in the way we communicate does not wave a magic wand over our relationship, but it creates small changes which can add up to something bigger. Incidentally, changing 'you' messages into 'I' messages can also have a very creative effect on the way we relate to our children.

Another discussion-stopper is our use of the words 'always' and 'never'. Because they are so total, there seems to be no point in challenging them. If you are repeatedly told that 'you never remember', it becomes a useless exercise to try. You then live down to this expectation!

When two people want something different, which affects them both, there are three ways in which they can handle it. In each case this can be a solution, or no solution, and that depends on the spirit of openness in which the discussion is held, and the love and respect that they have for each other.

Capitulation   The first way is capitulation. One side gives in. If the 'giving in' is in order to avoid conflict, then unexpressed resentment is going to remain and affect the couple's closeness. The one who capitulates may feel that their partner is trading upon their good nature, and yet they dare not say what they really want. They may even get a good feeling from doing the 'loving thing', but they are not giving their partner the chance to see the issue from another point of view.

A simple example of this might be seen in the behaviour of a wife who likes seaside holidays and whose husband prefers walking in the hills. Every time holidays are discussed she murmurs something about the sea being a possibility but never actually says that she would prefer that kind of holiday. She dare not spoil his holiday and might justify herself by saying, 'It doesn't really matter about me, as long as he's happy.' But of course it does matter to their relationship. It matters that her husband has the chance to give in for her sake. It matters that at times he tries to enter into her enjoyment and share it with her in the way that she does for him. If an open discussion takes place, each can say with equal strength what they like best. The one partner can still give way, but it can be acknowledged as generosity and accepted in love.

Coexistence   The second method of handling conflict is by coexistence. There is, of course, a great deal of mutual coexistence in marriage. Partners follow their own careers and often have some different interests. We can take a pleasure in our partner's enjoyment of something without necessarily wanting to be involved in it. We can see it as part of a comfortable balance between togetherness and separateness.

But coexistence in conflict is quite different. Here one or both of the partners is wanting a shared solution, but they cannot have it because neither feel that they can shift their ground with integrity.

This can happen over issues of great importance to us; a matter of principle, or a religious allegiance. It may be the point at which one partner will feel that their only option is to part company. Coexistence is too painful. Or they may try to handle it as best they can. How, in fact, do we love someone who appears to be thwarting us over something which matters to us a great deal? And is there any future in staying close to them in marriage when our values are different?

I think there are several factors here. The first is that though our values may be different in this one area, we were probably drawn together in the first place because our value systems were not so very different in other aspects. It is important that we do not let this one area of difference obscure other areas of togetherness. Secondly, we need to give each other credit for holding our different opinions with integrity. As in other matters we can never know the full history of the habits and hurts behind our partner's opinions. Thirdly, we need to recognize that our partner is not usually trying to hurt us. They just wish we could see it their way, and the difference hurts them too. However, neither of us can ease the other's pain without losing our integrity and that in itself would damage our relationship. Each of us needs to bear our own responsibility for causing pain to our partner.

Nothing which is alive is static. It is either growing or dying, and in showing respect and admitting our part in a shared pain, we are expressing love. This love does a hidden work in us which enables us to go on giving and receiving from one another. This works a change in us, and time will often show that we have learnt something from one another and connected more than we realized.

This happened to Paul and Louise. Paul was in the army when they got married and a few months later he was sent abroad. Unfortunately, it was not possible for various reasons for Louise to go with him, and they were apart for most of the next four years. After that Paul left the army and they were able to start a more normal life together. While in the army Paul had met a group of Christians who influenced his thinking. They showed him a working faith which seemed very relevant to him and quite different from the version he had learnt about at school. He decided to become a Christian and, when he left the army, he expected his wife to be equally enthused. She was not. This was not the man she had married. What right had he to try to change her? Why should she suddenly start going to church? It meant nothing to her. There followed some obvious conflict between them because Paul was longing to share his faith with Louise, and she longed for the closeness they had before he went into the army. But Paul began to realize that he must respect her opinions and he stopped trying to win her over. He committed his feelings and his wife to God out of love for them both. In a few months Louise began to see that Paul's faith mattered to him a great deal, and she wanted to be closer to him. She asked him to talk about it with her, and they did this together for several weeks. Soon after she decided to become a Christian herself.

For them the conflict was short-lived, but only because of Paul's ability to tolerate coexistence by continuing to respect Louise's right to be different. For others the difference between them may last a lifetime. Even so, the spirit in which they coexist can change an experience of hurt and loss into something which can enrich them both.

Coexistence can also be a way of not facing conflict. One partner can disconnect from the other in order that certain issues will not be raised. I have known this happen when a partner is jealous of the other's skill and does not want to be shown up, at sport for example.

It was also an early danger for my husband and me when I got married for the second time. I had become very practised at running the finances in my first marriage, and Paddy had been living at home where it was all done for him. Electricity bills were a whole new world! But Paddy wanted this role for himself and I was only too glad for him to have it. Even so, my past experience was a threat to him. Somehow we had to learn between us that, although my experience was of value, I did not know all the answers, and it was also all right for him to make mistakes. We had some fairly irritable exchanges, and if he had not been so determined he could easily have left it all to me. We would have avoided the conflict but we would have been much less happy with the end result.

We can disconnect from our partner because they embarrass us. Some people handle this by criticizing their partner in front of other people, hoping that this will shame them into changing. Our partner experiences this as disloyalty and our friends are often more embarrassed by our behaviour in exposing our partner than by that person's initial behaviour. Of course I am not talking about the teasing exchanges that are a normal part of conversation, but even jokes can be taken to the point of hurt, and if we pause for a moment we know when we are doing this. There are certain criticisms which need to be made in private if we are going to treat our partner with respect.

We can disconnect because we want to keep a group of friends to ourselves, and not let our partner come into the group. We need to ask ourselves some searching questions about why we feel this way. Our partner will certainly pick up any feelings of being excluded and want to know why. If it can be discussed both partners may be happy with the arrangement, or our partner might be included with our group of friends on occasions. If the situation cannot be discussed, that in itself is a disconnection.

Flirting can be used as a way of dealing with conflict by disconnecting from one's partner. It can be an expression of anger, or of punishment for some hurt. It may arise out of a need for reassurance, or to prove one's own attractiveness, but by involving someone else's feelings it gathers a momentum of its own, which is outside our own control. It is then much more difficult to discuss the original problem, and it can lead to a breakdown which was never a part of our original intention.

Compromise The third way of dealing with conflict is by compromise, and the bad face of compromise is an uneasy peace. No one gets what they want and both feel disgruntled and cheated.

But the word 'com-promise' comes from an origin which gives its happiest meaning. It means 'promising together'. When we meet each other halfway on any issue, each partner needs to recognize that both feel that they have given up their preferred way. If each person values the other person's sacrifice they will keep it in mind with an unspoken promise to respect it, and allow it to be fulfilled where possible. That is the expression of a loving relationship by compromise. If it is going to happen properly we need to know why our partner does not agree with us, and what they value which is different from us. Bad compromise comes out of bad communication, and good compromise out of good communication.

Strangely, we often handle big issues between us better than small ones, and sometimes we do not even realize what we are doing to each other. I knew a couple who had very different tastes in curtains, but they did not want to criticize each other. Both wanted to make their partner feel reasonably happy with their joint choices so neither felt free to express their true liking. Each felt that they were being very considerate towards the other, but every choice became an uncomfortable compromise which neither really liked. But another couple who liked very different paintings and said so took it in turns to choose a picture. They ended up with pictures which truly reflected their different personalities, and it happened that in time each grew to like most of their partner's choices. For them a happy compromise was found by taking it in turns to capitulate, and giving each other permission for both styles of picture to coexist!

Conflict touches our deepest feelings, and the more we are aware of our own feelings, the more we are likely to recognize them in others. Self-understanding is the first and biggest step towards understanding others. Though we will always be something of a mystery to ourselves, self-awareness is a skill which we can develop.

On several occasions I have taken part in a training exercise, designed to help people become more aware of the effect they can have on others. The participants are put into groups of five or six, and each person has a label placed on their forehead with a statement to the rest of the group. They do not know what their own label says, and they are not allowed to ask about it. The statements might read 'I'm important', 'I'm stupid', 'I'm a willing horse', 'I get angry quickly', 'Pity me', and so on. The group then discusses something general, such as how to improve public transport, and they answer each person as if the label that person has is true about them. Within ten minutes nearly everyone in the group has guessed their label from the way they are being treated, because they have begun to feel that way. After the exercise they will say, 'I began to feel very stupid because no one took any notice of my suggestions', or 'Everyone expected me to know the answer, I felt I was seen as the expert.'

The exercise demonstrates very powerfully that within a very short time a person can become the way others see him. The implications of this are very important to life in general, but especially to family life in all its many relationships. I am not suggesting that we should pretend that people are what they are not! But if we affirm a person's good qualities, it has a very constructive effect on them. Conversely, if we treat them as if we expect them to be bad-tempered, they will probably become more irritable. In other words, we have to take some responsibility for the way our partner behaves towards us. To some extent we make them that way.

If this affirmation can go hand in hand with recognizing the strength of the anger and hate which is in us all, we shall begin to get nearer the truth. And the truth is that we are all both much nicer and much nastier than we thought, and our

------

———

capacity for loving and hating is greater. We can also help one another and ourselves more than we sometimes realize.

Conflict. 'It's much worse than I thought.' This is a remark which I have heard couples say. They knew that marriage would bring its differences, but their own feels worse than they had expected. They also feel very alone with their conflicts, and unlike other couples. At the back of their minds is another thought, 'Are we normal?' To that I would usually want to answer, 'Yes.'

11

A new way of being loved

I have written so far without many references to my Christian faith, because I believe what I have said stands in its own right.

In my personal journey there have been times when my understanding of Christ's teaching has challenged my psychological understanding, and vice versa. As I have taken a closer look, I have usually found an underlying truth which has contained both, or I have recognized a difference which is one of language and interpretation. In fact truth cannot be at odds with itself.[1] There is a ring of truth which holds good wherever we find it, like the rings in a tree-trunk which run right through it.

I have also had to unlearn some distorted teaching and some half-truths and recognize in myself our ability to twist the truth for our own ends. Teaching is passed on through damaged human beings. Even the 'wisdom of God' has to be put into 'pots of clay'.[2] It is constantly handled and passed on through others like ourselves, and faith gets interwoven with fantasy in the process.

Whatever is taught cannot be received unless it can be understood, and we cannot understand something unless it can hook on to some little bit of knowledge, experience, or trust which we already have. For example, a little child, who received a mild shock while playing with an electric toy, said to his mother, 'It bit me!' He expressed the experience in terms of the only short, sharp pain he knew.

When we learn about a God who is 'Almighty' and 'Father', that hooks into our first experiences of authority and power, which we found in our parents. This touches emotions within us, some of which are deeply subconscious, which are a mixture of loving and hating, of trust and fear, and of warmth and anger. Gerard Hughes, who was for a while a chaplain at Glasgow University, said how important it was to know what kind of a God a student imagined before he suggested praying to him. The student might be imagining an ogre-like God with a big stick, or one who is usually absent, or one who does not really understand or care.[3]

Each of us comes to a working faith in God because we see in him something to which our spirit responds; he promises to meet some need in us. Inevitably our own needs will always be a mixture of 'neurotic' needs and true needs, but to us they are just needs. We see in God the possibility that a relationship with him might heal our past experience of love. In marriage too there is this same hope of redeeming the past, which is why we unconsciously set up the same problems we had as children. And so it is in our relationship with God.

If our parents seemed hard to please, and we often saw ourselves as a failure in their eyes, we will have a great desire to please God, who promises to accept us just as we are.[4] We will also want him to be very pleased with us. But just as we doubted the possibility of ever pleasing our demanding parents, so we will have a tendency to doubt the possibility of ever pleasing God. He will seem very hard to please. We are likely to believe that he is always more concerned about our sins and failures than anything else, and so will we be. We will feel driven to achieve a perfection we can never reach. Our eyes will gravitate to all the 'relevant' biblical passages and we will give them more weight than the comforting and accepting passages.

If we have grown up with an absent parent — and that could mean either physically or emotionally apart from us — we may well have grown up blaming ourselves for it, in the irrational belief that it was because we were not lovable

------

enough. Then our God, who promises to 'never leave us or forsake us'[5] will not just be temporarily hidden from our sight by a cloud of depression or difficulty, but will seem to have gone away and left us to look after ourselves.

If we have often felt misunderstood as children, we will be drawn to a God who knows the thoughts of our heart even before we speak,[6] but when as adults we feel misunderstood, we will not easily call to mind the possibility of prayer or think of resting in God's understanding of us, because in those moments we do not expect him to understand. In fact, because most of us have experienced all these negative feelings at times, our own picture of God will be distorted by them. The kind of God we have created through our fantasies will also be limited by them.

But Christ's relationship with his Father provides me with a yardstick against which to measure my own internal images of God, and of the nature of love. This means that I am constantly having to make comparisons between love as I have experienced it and the love which I see in the life of Jesus Christ. As I look at him I see someone who loved out of the fullness of his sense of being loved by God. He knew himself to be the 'beloved Son',[7] able to rest 'in the bosom of the Father'.[8] He said to his disciples, 'I love you in the way that my Father loves me, and I want you to be able to love one another by drawing on my love for you. I want you to experience a new way of being loved and so find a new way of loving.'[9]

The reason why Jesus loved his disciples could not have been because they were good. They tempted him. 'Get thee behind me, Satan!'[10] Jesus said one day to Peter. The disciples doubted Jesus' word. They betrayed him. They were unsupportive. 'Could you not keep watch for one hour?'[11] he asked them; but he could not count on them to stay awake as he wrestled in prayer at the prospect of death on a cross. At the crucifixion only the women stayed close by. Jesus was always straight with his friends, and on some occasions he rebuked

------

them, but he loved them. It overflowed from his Father's love for him. Even when he was on the cross he could say, 'Father, forgive them, for they know not what they do'.[12] Who 'they' were we shall never know. Was it the soldiers who nailed him to the cross, or the authorities who gave the orders, or the disciples who could not face staying near by? I suspect that it would have been all three groups.

Jesus had felt the same way when he spoke about Jerusalem, with deep longings for a city full of people who did not want to hear what he had to tell them about the depth of God's love for them.[13] They mistrusted the love of God, as we all do, seeing it as manipulating, or demanding obedience to a set of religious rules, tyrannical or irrelevant. We learned from a very early age that we have to be good to be loved by the God we have imagined. Therefore we find it hard to believe the good news that God is not like that. The mother/father God whom Christ knew was one who 'gathered her chickens under her wings',[14] who saw the potential he had created in each individual and loved that creation. He was the God who had with Christ a real, adult father/son relationship of love and trust, so that each was fully themselves, yet in unity with the other in their shared Spirit.

There is no way that a couple of fallen human beings can ever reach that state in their relationship, but to the extent that one or both of them can rest in Christ's love for them, they can have an added resource for their relationship. This gives them greater possibilities for breaking their bondage to their past broken experiences. Even the old Prayer Book marriage service points this out in its introductory paragraph: 'Marriage signifies the mystical union that is betwixt Christ and His church.' That union is for the redemption of society and the individual.

But every time we look at an 'ideal' situation, we have to look at the reality of where we are and who we are. We are broken people, trespassers and trespassed against. We fail and lack trust, and will continue to do so. We have hearts that know about hate as well as love. In all our marriages we fail ourselves and one another, and divorce is there because our pain is sometimes too great to bear. There is a limit in all of us beyond which we cannot stay in a relationship and this is our reality. The bearing of nastiness, our partner's and our own, is too painful. It makes us feel too unloved and unlovable.

The good news in this situation is that God has shown us through the cross that even our 'nastiness' need not break our relationship with him. I had a friend many years ago who was a Jewish agnostic child psychotherapist, and it happened that one day we got into a conversation about Christianity. She said that she did not want to look at Christianity because of all the suffering which the Jewish people had experienced at the hands of Christians down the centuries, but that she saw in the cross a true picture of the nature of love. I asked her what made her say that and she replied, 'Sometimes I see a child having a tantrum in a department store, and the mother is unable to bear the shame which her child is causing her. The glances and tut-tuts of onlookers either make her try to ignore the child in an attempt to disown it, or be harder on the child than it deserves. But at other times I see a mother who can bear her child's rage or distress within herself, and then she responds to the child out of their mutual relationship, being as soft or as firm as she feels is most helpful to the child in that moment. This is an expression of a sacrificial and creative love, which can accept and bear the "bad" in a person as a part of their whole person, and this helps them to grow.'

I found this a very moving comparison which helped me in two ways. It gave me an ideal to strive for as a mother, and a picture of a God who could bear me when I failed as a mother and still love me. It made the meaning of the cross of Christ very alive for me.

It will take us all our lives to unlearn our deep conviction that we have to earn God's love in order to be acceptable to him. For this process to happen we have to give God some space for our relationship with him, just as we have to spend time with our partner in order to call it a marriage. We need to learn ways of listening to his 'still, small voice'[15] within us. We need to read the Bible intelligently and with humility in order to find out what kind of a relationship God the Father had with his Son, and what he wants to have with us. We need to be honest and vulnerable with him in prayer, telling him about our good and bad thoughts and feelings. It is often in the expression of our bad feelings that we find a new peacefulness. This sort of conversation with God is shown in the following poem written by a patient in Broadmoor and published in the in-house magazine.

> When the stars are shining at night
> And I can't sleep right,
> Put a cloak of calm round me,
> Jesus, put a cloak of calm round me,
> Put a cloak of calm round me.
>
> When my nerves are bad
> And I am feeling bad,
> And the day is long, and everything is wrong,
> Put a cloak of calm round me,
> Jesus, put a cloak of calm round me,
> Put a cloak of calm round me.
>
> When I am bad and everyone seems glad,
> When the voices are bad
> And I feel quite mad,
> Put a cloak of calm round me,
> Jesus, put a cloak of calm round me,
> Put a cloak of calm round me.
>
> Peter Morrow[16]

———

I feel sure that after writing this the author did feel something of the peace of God. Even the act of framing those thoughts into a poem would have made it more real for him and strengthened his faith.

It is as our relationship with God develops that we come up against our muddled and conflicting pictures of him. In our 'first love' for him things often look clear and straightforward. So it is with marriage. Difficulties show themselves when we are actually living in the relationship, and particularly when we are under stress, unwell, or tired.

Being a Christian does not protect a marriage from any of the normal pressures of life. It may help us through difficulties but not round them. It may even give us some additional problems as we wrestle with the tension between an ideal to aim at and a reality to live with, and as we confront some of our fantasies.

I believe that the marriages of those who are in high profile church jobs — such as clergy couples, church workers, and youth club leaders — are especially at risk from this kind of tension. In fact anyone who makes a public statement of faith is open to criticism for not living up to their ideal. Though we know ourselves to be fallible human beings we can get seduced into putting too high an expectation on ourselves and our partners, and we then feel under pressure from our own and other people's fantasies about the kind of role we 'ought' to fulfil. Marriages with great potential can break down under these conditions, and sad to say they sometimes do. The very fact of feeling different and 'on a pedestal' removes the couple from the normal human friendships which might have helped them through their difficulties.

I have been told that at some theological colleges clergy are advised not to make close friendships within the parish, because this might cause jealousy. Of course such friendships need to be handled sensitively. But I do wonder why God should have gone to such great lengths to show us how he lives in human flesh and blood if he wanted to support us entirely through a direct line from his Spirit to ours. The pattern we have is of Jesus living vulnerably among his friends. To be deprived of human friendship is to be a deprived person. Some church workers and clergy work so hard six days a week, and in places so far away from their friends or relations, that these non-local friendships cannot be maintained. Then their marriages are much more at risk than others.

Of course that can be equally true for any marriage where one partner is almost totally caught up in their work. I have heard wives say that they feel more like a mistress than a wife, because their husband is actually wedded to his work and not to them. And the converse is true, that wives can draw their children around them in a way that excludes the husband and father, leaving him feel like a spare part. In fact these two situations often go together, each giving rise to the other.

But an additional difficulty for those in church work is that they sometimes find it hard to distinguish between their devotion to God and their responsibility to the church as an organization. I am very glad to see an increase in the support being offered to clergy couples and other such families, as they bear a great burden from society's expectations of them. This is also true for people in the caring professions, and many Christians are drawn into these careers by their desire to serve God and the community.

One of the greatest differences that a faith in Christ can bring to a marriage is in the area of hope. Even though a couple may bring all that they have to their marriage there will be times when both are needy and neither feel they have anything to give. Faith in an outside resource is a very real hope. We are not operating in a closed system. Someone from outside ourselves can come in and change things. I remember a wife saying that although she was furious with her husband, when she saw him praying she found herself saying to God, 'Well, I can't do anything more, maybe you can do something to change him!' and as she said it she realised that the same might be true for her.

Christian hope is not a false hope in a fantasy which says, 'It doesn't matter how bad things are, it will all come right in the end.' It is the hope God gives us by taking into account all that we are, the messes we have made, and the circumstances we are in, and saying to us, 'Well, where shall we go from here, you and I together?' It is a way of possibilities which says, 'Today is the first day of the rest of your life'. It is a yet-to-be-discovered way. And God's own desire to accompany us along the way gives importance and meaning to our lives. We are a part of something very much bigger than ourselves, which gives us a new worth.

12

Conclusion

Working with married couples has kept me very aware of how little anyone can know from the outside about the facts and fantasies of other people's relationships. Counsellors, pastors and psychotherapists are often seen by those who are asking for help as people with X-ray eyes. That is a fantasy in itself. The helpers too are not without their own fantasies about themselves and those they help.

Christ has been called the 'wounded healer', and that name also seems to embody the best that any of us can be to one another. But the greatest 'worker' in the building-up of a relationship is undoubtedly the person in the centre of it. Theirs is the journey of courage and of patience, through hopes and disappointments, but theirs too is the real gain.

The following poem sums up for me the attitude of heart and mind which contributes most to self-discovery and good relationships.

> Learn to know the mind-behind-
> Mind that sees when you are blind.
> Learn to trust the mind-below-
> Mind that's wiser than you know.
>
> Learn to meet the fear you fear,
> Hate you hate, and see them clear.
> Enter the forbidden place.
> Face at last your other face.

Conclusion

Learn to be alone; then only
Reach out hand no longer lonely.
Grow, be tall yet reconciled
To yourself, the weeping child.

Love; be easy, and be warm.
Find the fire beyond the form.
Laugh. Forgive yourself; forgive
Sins long dead, and learn to live.

A. S. J. Tessimond[1]

Notes

2 THE SEED-BED OF OUR EMOTIONS

1 John Milton (1608–1674), *Paradise Regained*, IV, 1.220 (1671).
2 Frank Lake, *Tight Corners in Counselling* (Darton, Longman and Todd 1981).
3 Psalm 139.1, 4, 6, 13, 16, 17.
4 John 4.10. (AV)
5 C.S. Lewis (1898–1963), *Mere Christianity* (Bles 1952).
6 A.A. Milne (1882–1956), *Now We Are Six* (Methuen 1927).

3 THE CHOICE OF A PARTNER

1 Robin Skynner and John Cleese, *Families and How to Survive Them* (Methuen 1983).
2 Proverbs 20.5 (adapted).

4 'DON'T BLAME ME!'

1 Sherwood and Glidewell, the 'Pinch/Crunch' chart (redrawn).
2 Common misquotation from Germaine Necker de Staël (1766–1817), *Corinne or Italy* (1807), 18, 5.
3 1 Corinthians 13.12 (AV, adapted).
4 The Lord's Prayer from The Alternative Service Book 1980 © The Central Board of Finance of the Church of England.

5 CLOSENESS AND SEPARATENESS

1 Robert Browning (1812–1889), 'Two in the Campagna' in *Men and Women* (1855).
2 C. Day Lewis (1904–1972), taken from 'Marriage of two?' published in *The Complete Poems of C. Day Lewis*, ed. Jill Balcon (Sinclair Stevenson 1992).
3 John Donne (1572–1631), 'The Good-Morrow' in *John Donne* (The Oxford Authors) ed. John Carey (Oxford University Press 1990).
4 Robert Graves (1895–1985), 'Call It a good marriage' in *Collected Poems* (1975). Reprinted by permission of A.P. Watt Ltd,

on behalf of the Executors of the Estate of Robert Graves and Oxford University Press Inc, New York: copyright © 1954 New Directions.

5   Dylan Thomas (1914–1953), *Under Milk Wood* (Dent 1954).
6   Kahlil Gibran, *The Prophet* (Heinemann 1926).
7   Roger and Donna Vann, *Secrets of a Growing Marriage* (Hodder and Stoughton 1985).
8   John Donne, *Devotions Upon Emergent Occasions*, 17 (1624) in *John Donne* (The Oxford Authors).
9   Dietrich Bonhoeffer (1906–1945), *Life Together* (SCM Press 1954).

6   LOVING AND LOSING

1   Alfred, Lord Tennyson (1809–1892), *In Memoriam*, XXVIII (1850).

7   SEX AND GENDER

1   H.F. Harlow and R.R. Zimmerman, 'Affectional Responses in Infant Monkeys', *Science* (1959), 130:421–32; H.F. Harlow, J.L. McGaragh and R.F. Thompson, *Psychology* (San Francisco: Albion 1971); W.T. McKinney, 'Psychoanalysis Revisited in Terms of Experimental Primatology' in E.T. Adelson (ed.) *Sexuality and Psychoanalysis* (New York: Brunner/Mazel 1975).

8   CHILDREN OF OUR GENERATION

1   Michael Aspel on *Aspel on Sunday* (Easter Day, April 11, 1993).
2   Karl Marx (1818–1883), from a letter to his wife, Jenny, when she was visiting her dying mother in Trier, dated June 21, 1856. Quoted in *The Oxford Book of Marriage*, ed. Helge Rubinstein (Oxford University Press 1991).
3   John 12.24.
4   Song of Songs 1.13, 15, 16; 2.7; 3.5.

11   A NEW WAY OF BEING LOVED

1   See Matthew 12.25–8.
2   See 2 Corinthians 4.7.
3   Gerard Hughes, *In Search of a Way* (Darton, Longman and Todd 1978).

4   Luke 23.43.
5   Matthew 28.20.
6   Psalm 139.4.
7   Matthew 3.17.
8   John 1.18 AV.
9   John 15.9 (author's paraphrase).
10 Mark 8.33 AV.
11 Mark 14.37.
12 Luke 23.34 AV.
13 Deuteronomy 32.11.
14 Matthew 23.37.
15 1 Kings 19.12 AV.
16 Peter Morrow in Broadmoor in-house magazine, September 1978.

12   CONCLUSION

1   A.S.J. Tessimond (1902–1962), 'The Psychiatrist's Song' from *Voices in a Giant City* (Heinemann 1947).

Also published by

Tri∧nglE

FACING ANXIETY
by Roy Ward

An exploration of the causes of anxiety and its effects on our lives. Roy Ward offers practical suggestions for coping with anxiety.

UNDERSTANDING FRIENDS
How to get the best out of friendship
by Alistair Ross
Foreword by David Atkinson

Alistair Ross examines the many complex and fascinating questions involved in our relationships, including our ability to sympathize with others.

LIVING WITH ANGER
by Myra Chave-Jones

Takes a positive view of anger and how it can be used as an important part of our lives.

FREE TO FAIL
by Russ Parker

A Christian exploration of the problems many people have with facing up to failure and its place in the spiritual life.

SEVEN FOR A SECRET THAT'S NEVER BEEN TOLD
Healing the wounds of sexual abuse in childhood
by Tracy Hansen

A moving account of a survivor of child sexual abuse working through the trauma induced by the return of repressed memories.

IMPOSSIBLE DECISIONS
Making decisions when no way seems right
by Doreen Padfield, with Deborah Padfield

A down-to-earth look at decisions where, whatever we do, someone will be hurt. The book finds common features in routine choices as well as major dilemmas.

FROM WHERE I SIT
Living with disability in an able-bodied world
by Alison Davis

A disturbing, personal and often funny account of what it is really like to be disabled.

WHO'S THIS SITTING IN MY PEW?
Mentally handicapped people in the church
by Faith Bowers

Considers what the church can do for mentally handicapped people and what they bring to the church.

BEGINNING WHERE I AM
Meditations for young people
by Godfrey Holmes

Meditations and prayers for a wide range of modern situations, with suggestions for beginning your own prayer life.

TRI△NGLE

Books
can be obtained from
all good bookshops.
In case of difficulty,
or for a complete list of our books,
contact:
SPCK Mail Order
36 Steep Hill
Lincoln
LN2 1LU
(tel: 0522 527 486)